Mary Anning

and **Paleontology** for **Kids**

HER LIFE AND DISCOVERIES, WITH 21 ACTIVITIES

Stephanie Bearce

CHICAGO REVIEW PRESS

Published by Chicago Review Press Incorporated
814 North Franklin Street
Chicago, Illinois 60610
ISBN 978-1-64160-833-6

Library of Congress Control Number: 2024932322

Cover and interior design: Sarah Olson
Cover images: (front, clockwise from upper left) portrait of
Mary Anning, courtesy of Wikimedia Commons; southwest
coast of England, Otto Borik/Shutterstock.com; engraving of
plesiosaurus skeleton, Andrii_Oliinyk/stock.adobe.com; *Duria
Antiquior*, painted in 1830 by geologist Henry De la Beche,
courtesy of Wikimedia Commons; drawing of ichthyosaur
skull found by Joseph and Mary Anning, courtesy of Wikimedia
Commons; large ammonite, photo by Darrell Bearce, courtesy
of the Lyme Regis Museum; (back, clockwise from upper left)
large fossil, Nazmus/stock.adobe.com; fossilized ichthyosaur
skeleton, Sombra/Shutterstock.com; shell fossils, Semnic/
Shutterstock.com
Illustrations: Jim Spence

Every effort has been made to contact the copyright holders
for the images that appear in this book. The publisher would
welcome information concerning any inadvertent errors or
omissions.

Printed in the United States of America

For Darrell, my favorite adventure partner

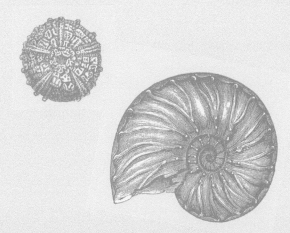

Contents

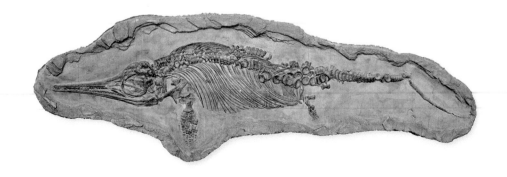

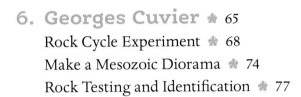

Time Line

1665 Robert Hook uses microscope to compare fossils to living organisms

1676 Femur of a *Megalosaurus* discovered in England, incorrectly identified as a giant human

1764–1766 Fossilized bones of huge lizard found in the Netherlands

1789 Skeleton of giant sloth uncovered in Argentina

1796 Joseph Anning is born

Georges Cuvier argues the reality of extinction

1799 Mary Anning is born in Lyme Regis, England

1800 Cuvier identifies the first pterodactyl

Mary Anning survives a lightning strike

1807 The Geological Society of London is formed

1810 Richard Anning dies

1811 Joseph and Mary Anning find *Ichthyosaurus* skull

1812 Mary Anning excavates body belonging to the skull

1818 William Buckland named the first reader (professor) in geology at Oxford

1821 William Buckland finds hyena den containing bones of lions, elephants, and rhinoceroses

1823 Mary Anning discovers first complete plesiosaur

1824 William Buckland presents first scientific paper to describe a dinosaur, the massive *Megalosaurus*

Mary Anning deduces that bezoar stones are fossilized feces

1826 Mary Anning opens her shop on Broad Street

1828 Mary Anning discovers the first British pterosaur

1829 Mary Anning finds the first *Squaloraja* fossil

Mary Anning visits London

1830 Henry De la Beche publishes *Duria Antiquior*

Mary excavates complete plesiosaur fossil now displayed at British Natural History Museum

1831 Charles Darwin departs on the five-year voyage that will help him develop the concept of evolution

Introduction

Today Mary Anning is known around the world as being the girl who discovered **dinosaurs**. But during Mary's lifetime, she worked in relative obscurity. A self-educated woman who grew up in poverty in the rural town of Lyme Regis, England, Mary had to work hard to earn a living in a job that was dominated by men.

During the 1800s, no English universities were open to women, but even if they were, they would not have been available to Mary. Born into the lower class of British society, her abilities were questioned not only because she was female but also because of her social status.

Determined to make a living doing the work she loved, Mary spent hours reading every scientific article she could get her hands on. She taught herself how to draw and illustrated her **fossil** specimens for her customers and interested scientists. She became an expert in animal anatomy and was able to put together **fossilized** skeletons accurately at a time when the animals were still new to science.

Financially, Mary was able to improve both her life and that of her mother, moving them out of an often-flooded poor section of town to a nicer home with a storefront window. At times she struggled to maintain her financial independence, but friends who admired her work came to her assistance.

Scientists like William Buckland, Henry De la Beche, and William Conybeare depended on Mary's expertise to supply them and their museums with fossil specimens, yet at the same time they often neglected to give her credit for her outstanding work. Recognition has come only recently, as historians have traced the history of ichthyosaur and plesiosaur fossils back to the young woman in Lyme Regis.

It took years of protests, feminist movements, and thankless work by female pioneers like Mary Anning to break the social barriers. In 1868, more than 20 years after Mary's death, the University of London voted to allow women to sit for their General Examination.

Today, more than 200 years since Mary was born, there are women at all levels of study in higher education. Women with doctorates in paleontology lead field teams to dig and discover new fossils. They teach classes at universities around the world and write groundbreaking research papers. Mary Anning would be proud to see her sister fossilists breaking barriers and changing science.

1

The Girl Who Loved Fossils

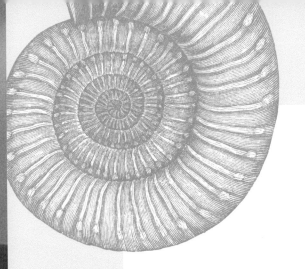

The girl scrambled across the rocky cliffs, fossil sack slung over her shoulder, wind whipping her long skirt. Her eyes scanned the hill, looking for a glint of bone in the piles of limestone and shale. She paid no attention to the roar of waves crashing on the shore below. Her eyes were trained to see **vertebrae** frozen in stone and giant teeth buried in gravel. Her name was Mary Anning. She was one of the best dinosaur hunters in the world, and she was only 12 years old.

The famous Jurassic Coast is the source of millions of fossil specimens.
Photo by Darrell Bearce, courtesy of the photographer

Ancient Cobb and harbor of Lyme Regis. *Photo by Darrell Bearce, courtesy of the photographer*

Mary Anning was born on May 21, 1799, on the rugged English coast in the town of Lyme Regis. She was a scrawny slip of a child, so small and weak nobody expected her to live. Her parents, Richard and Mary "Molly" Anning, wrapped the baby in blankets and tried to keep the fire going in their tiny home. Maybe if they kept young Mary warm, she would survive.

The Annings were a poor working-class family who lived in the lower part of Lyme Regis, called Cockamoile Square. Homes in this area were small, cramped, and so close to the ocean that they often flooded. Bone-chilling winds whipped through the cracks in the walls. Keeping warm was a struggle. There was certainly no money to pay for a doctor.

Even if they could have hired the services of a doctor, it wouldn't have done much good. The best healing agents 19th-century medicine had to offer were potions made from herbs and dangerous chemical mixtures containing cocaine and opium. Like many people of that time, the Annings had already buried four children. Their one surviving child was three-year-old Joseph. With only small hope that the baby would survive, they gave her the name Mary after a sister who had died earlier. Perhaps this Mary would beat the odds.

Lightning Strikes

Mary Anning proved to be a stubborn girl. At 15 months she was still in sickly health with a perpetual cough and poor appetite, but she was alive. A local nurse, Elizabeth Hodgkins, was a friend of the family and often checked on Mary. One warm day in August 1800, Elizabeth offered to take the toddler on an outing to give her some fresh air, and probably to give her mother, Molly, a break from the fussy little one. Molly Anning agreed, and soon Mary and Elizabeth were enjoying a Sunday afternoon at a horse show.

Lyme Regis was a tourist town because of the man-made harbor called the Cobb. This curving seawall, built in the 1200s, provided the town with a large body of calm water perfect for ships and the tourists who wanted to try out the new health craze called sea bathing. Wealthy people from around England flocked to towns like Lyme Regis to spend time in the ocean exercising and drinking large doses of seawater. During the summer months, traveling shows came to town to entertain the tourists and earn some money. Troupes of

BATHING MACHINES

Today almost everybody loves swimming. Splashing in a pool or floating in the ocean is a great way to cool off and have fun. But in the 1800s it was considered improper for a woman to let any man see her bare ankles. Heaven forbid a man saw a calf or a thigh! In this age of modesty, women had to wear dresses even when they were swimming. And they couldn't change into their bathing dress and walk down to the beach. Someone might see them. Oh, what a scandal!

To protect the women's modesty and allow them to enjoy the ocean, hotels and beaches provided bathing machines. The machine was a shed placed on wheels and hauled by a horse or mule. While on the beach, a woman could climb into the shed and change into her bathing costume.

Once she was in her bathing dress and her regular clothes were stored in a compartment on the roof, the horse would pull the shed out into the water. The woman could then discreetly step into the ocean and swim.

But swimming in a heavy dress was difficult. The wet fabric made it impossible to float, and most ladies never had swimming lessons. The owners of the bathing machines usually tied a rope around the swimmers' waists. That way if a lady started to drown, she could be easily pulled in.

Illustration of a Victorian bathing machine. *Courtesy of Wikimedia Commons*

singers, comedy players, and horse shows were a lovely way for both the rich and poor to spend an afternoon.

That August afternoon seemed like many others. The crowd cheered the horses as they raced and jumped. Elizabeth sat with little Mary under the shade of a huge old tree. She chatted with two of her friends, learning about the town gossip and talking about the beautiful horses. The ladies were dressed in their nicest clothes, which meant long full skirts that reached below their ankles, good sturdy lace-up boots, and shirtwaists with sleeves that fully covered their arms to the wrist. Of course, they were wearing bonnets to cover their heads and shield their faces from the sun. With such heavy clothing, it was no wonder Elizabeth and her friends stayed in the shade all afternoon.

As the day wore on, clouds built up over the ocean. Then suddenly the winds picked up and the sky grew dark. A deafening crash shook the ground. The smell of scorched wood and burnt flesh filled the air. The tree where Elizabeth and Mary sat lay in splintered pieces.

Frantic friends and neighbors rushed to help, but it was too late. Lightning traveling through the tree roots had electrocuted the three women. Their bonnets and ruffled shirts were burnt and the soles of their boots blown off like firecrackers.

Horrified, townspeople tried to revive the women, when miraculously one man noticed little Mary still clutched in the dead arms of Elizabeth Hodgkins. He scooped the toddler up and listened for a heartbeat. Mary was alive.

The man ran from the show grounds back to the center of town to the Annings' home. There Mary's frantic parents did what they could. They gave their baby a warm bath, wrapped her in blankets, and once again hoped for the best. Incredibly, she not only survived but thrived.

Fossils with Father

From that point on, Mary seemed to have a new lease on life. The toddler grew into a strong girl who relished spending time outdoors, following her father and brother as they hiked along the trails of Lyme Regis. The cliffs beside Lyme Bay were made of a combination of soft shale and limestone.

Crinoid fossils. *Courtesy of kevinzim / Kevin Walsh, Wikimedia Commons, https://commons.wikimedia.org/wiki /File:Crinoid_Fossils_of_Jurassic.jpg*

THUNDERBOLTS AND SNAKESTONES

The early fossil collectors of Lyme Regis didn't know what made the strange rocks that were scattered across their beaches. Some people thought they were beautiful decorations that God allowed to bubble up to the Earth's surface, much like a flower or tree grew from a seed. Others believed they were the remains of plants and animals that died in the Old Testament flood.

Locals named the stones according to their shape. Long, skinny pointed fossils were called *thunderbolts* and were believed to have been created when lightning struck the ground. People also believed that the thunderbolt had medicinal properties. Powdered thunderbolts were used to treat eye infections in horses. To cure a horse of worms people soaked thunderbolts in water and then fed the water to the horse. Scientists have since discovered that the thunderbolts are the fossilized bodies of an extinct squid-like animal called a belemnite.

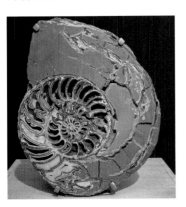

Another popular fossil was the *snakestone*, which looked like a snake curled into a circle. Snakestones were thought to have the power to cure all sorts of problems, including poisonings and snakebites. They were often worn as an amulet to ward off evil. Scientists have identified the snakestone as the fossilized shell of the ammonite. It is an extinct **cephalopod** that swam in the ancient seas that covered Lyme Regis.

Ammonites and belemnites are still valued by fossil collectors today. They are often polished and made into jewelry or put on display, much like the souvenirs the Annings sold.

Fossilized ammonite. *Photo by Darrell Bearce, courtesy of the British Natural History Museum*

This made the cliffs treacherous, since a strong wave or storm could cause the cliffs to crumble. But the cliffs also held amazing treasures.

In the late 1700s and early 1800s, people loved to collect specimens from nature. Feathers, seashells, interesting rocks, and even taxidermy were proudly displayed in the parlors and libraries of wealthy people. They collected these specimens on their travels to places like Bath and Lyme Regis.

Richard Anning had moved to Lyme Regis from a small town called Sidbury to work as a cabinetmaker. The burgeoning tourism in Lyme Regis

The cliffs of Lyme Regis where Mary Anning prospected for fossils.
Photo by Darrell Bearce, courtesy of the photographer

was increasing the town's population, and Richard knew that more people meant more potential business. But when Richard arrived at Lyme Regis, he became fascinated with the unusual rock formations. His wife, Molly, thought the fossils took too much of his time and hurt his cabinet business. But Richard realized tourists were willing to pay for rocks and shells to take home as souvenirs, and spending days hiking on the coast and wandering the hills was much more exciting than days inside working as a carpenter. Richard set himself up as a seller of rare and unusual rock specimens and became a familiar figure striding up and down the area's beaches and scrambling up the rocky hills.

Each day as the tide rushed in, it washed out new layers of rock. In these rocks were strange shells and pieces of bone. People called them fossils, but at that time the definition of a fossil was anything that had been dug out of the earth. Nobody understood where these shells and bones came from or why they were buried in the rocks around Lyme Regis.

Most people assumed that the fossils were a result of the great flood written about in the Old Testament of the Bible—that the animals who were not saved by Noah and his ark died, and their bodies were buried in the mud from the flood. People believed that was why they found seashells, shark teeth, and animal bones on mountainsides and on cliffs above the ocean. Scientists who offered alternative explanations were dismissed by religious leaders.

By the time Mary was six years old, she was an experienced fossil hunter. Always happy to

Make a Fossil

The fossils Mary and her father collected were created millions of years ago when animals died and were covered by sediments and soil. The skin and inner organs of the animal decomposed, leaving the hard bones and teeth behind. Over time, the bones were covered by soil and minerals and hardened into rock, or **petrified.**

Fossils can also be created by **molds**, or casts. The original bone or shell dissolves and leaves an empty space called a mold. The space is filled in with minerals and sediments to form a matching cast. Many shells, octopuses, and squid are found as casts, because their shells dissolve easily.

You can create a fossil mold using this recipe.

MATERIALS

- ⭐ 1 cup salt
- ⭐ 3 cups flour
- ⭐ 1 cup brewed coffee (cold)
- ⭐ 2 cups used coffee grounds
- ⭐ Mixing bowl
- ⭐ Mixing spoon
- ⭐ Wax paper
- ⭐ Objects to make fossil impressions (ex: shells, plastic animal models for footprints or skin impressions, stiff leaves, twigs, etc.)

1. Combine the salt, flour, brewed coffee, and coffee grounds in the mixing bowl. Stir until smooth. If the mixture is too wet, add flour to achieve a firm consistency.

2. Spread this dough out on wax paper in several places. Flatten each piece to the thickness of a cookie.

3. Select shells, twigs, or animals to press into the dough. These will make the fossil prints.

4. Press each object firmly into a dough piece and remove it carefully. Leave the dough to dry and create the fossils. Drying may take two to five days depending on humidity. But it's much faster than the million years or so that it takes to make a real fossil.

abandon the boring household tasks of washing and scrubbing, she eagerly combed the beaches with her father and brother. They set out early in the morning, cloth sacks slung over their shoulders with rock picks stashed inside. Richard made a small pick just the right size for his daughter's little hands. Together they searched for the round brachiopods that tumbled in the rolling waves. Mary would run out and grab the stones just before they rolled out to sea.

Ammonites, curled fossilized shells, were a special treasure. Richard knew how to slice the shells in half to expose their beautiful crystallized interior. These stones were prized by collectors. Money from selling them helped provide food and shelter for the Anning family.

Once their sacks were full of fossilized treasures, the Anning team returned home to Richard's workshop and cleaned their bounty. Mary learned how to use a small brush and needle to clear away any extra pieces of rock that covered the fossil. The cleaner and more pristine the fossil, the more the tourists would pay. Once the fossils were cleaned and polished, they were put on display on a large round table outside the Anning home.

A natural salesman, Richard knew how to sweet talk the customers and taught Mary the art of negotiating the best deal. Richard also taught his children some of his cabinetmaking skills. They built beautiful wooden boxes that tourists could purchase to display their fossils and shells.

Mother's Objections

Molly Anning was not thrilled that her daughter was a fossil hunter. Girls were supposed to learn the skills of housekeeping. In the early 1800s, most women were expected to marry and take care of a house and family. That was seen as the proper job for a woman. Molly worried that her daughter would be considered strange and wild. She'd never find a husband and would be left a spinster. The job options for single women were very few. She could be a domestic worker for a wealthy family or work in the fish markets cleaning and selling fish.

Mary couldn't care less about being a proper young lady, but she did spend time helping her mother with washing, weaving rush mats,

The site of the Dissenters church the Anning family attended.
Photo by Darrell Bearce, courtesy of the photographer

preserving food, and learning how to manage a home. However, her heart was always on the cliffs and shore, imagining the next wonderful fossil find.

Richard encouraged Mary's adventurous spirit. A bit of a rebel himself, Richard was a member of the Dissenters church. Its followers opposed government interference in religious matters and broke away from the state-sponsored Church of England. Many Dissenters formed their own churches, and some of them immigrated to Canada and the United States.

The Dissenters church in Lyme Regis provided religious instruction and taught its members how

GETTING SCHOOLED

When Mary Anning was a child, school was only for the wealthy. Educating the poor was not a priority, and there were no free public schools. Wealthy British families paid for private classes and teachers or sent their children to boarding school. Lower-class families needed their youngsters to go to work as early as possible to help pay for food and shelter.

Most children worked six days a week on farms, factories, and boat docks. Five-year-olds were hired by factories as equipment cleaners and spent their days darting in and out of the fast-moving machines. Their fingers were able to reach in cracks and crevices that were too small for adult hands. Cleaning while the equipment was in operation led to many injuries, and some children were killed, but factory owners thought it was too costly to turn off the machines simply to clean them. Children were considered disposable, and there were no laws to protect them.

Mary and her brother Joseph were some of the lucky few who were able to get an education. They attended a Sunday school sponsored by their church. Volunteer teachers met with students for five hours every Sunday, teaching reading, writing, and math. The classes were free to anyone who wanted to attend and were open to adults as well as children.

Students practiced writing and solved math problems using a piece of polished slate fit inside a wood frame. They wrote with a clay pencil and cleaned the board with a rag after the teacher approved their work. Paper and ink were far too expensive. Most schools used the Bible to practice reading, but some did have books called *primers* that had simple sentences to help beginning readers.

In the late 1800s, both Great Britain and America realized that educating children was important to society. Lawmakers allocated money to build schools, and children from the ages of 6 to 10 were required to attend. It was an important change in how children were treated.

to read, write, and understand mathematics. This was the only formal education Mary and Joseph received, because in the 1800s England did not have a free public school system.

The rhythm of Mary's life was set: helping her mother with necessary work some days and other days traipsing with her father through the waves and over the hills. On Sundays, she spent six hours at church learning about God, arithmetic, and letters. It felt peaceful, but it was not always safe.

The waves and storms that hit the Lyme Regis coast often caused landslides. This revealed new fossils, but it was also dangerous. It was after one of these storms that Richard Anning eagerly went out to see what new wonders had been exposed. The earth beneath his feet shifted and fell. Richard crashed to the ground with the rocks. He managed to return home, but he never fully recovered.

Richard Anning died in 1810 when Mary was just 11 and her brother Joseph was 14. With her father's death, Mary's life changed forever.

Landslide!

*Land areas made of **sedimentary rocks** are prone to landslides when exposed to storms and waves. Mary Anning's father died due to injuries he experienced during a landslide, and Mary dodged death and injury several times.*
    You can experiment to see how water affects hills and causes landslides.

MATERIALS

- 2 plastic tubs
- Gravel
- Sand
- Potting soil
- Watering can filled with water

1. Use one of the plastic tubs to hold your hill. Fill one half of the bottom of the tub with a layer of gravel at least an inch (25 mm) thick, leaving the other half empty. Next, pour an inch of sand on top of the gravel and pack it firmly. Cover the sand with an inch of soil and pack it firmly.

2. Repeat the layers until you have covered half of the tub up to the top of the rim. The other half should remain empty. This is where you will place the water for ocean erosion. Water erosion can be caused by too much rain, or it can result from moving bodies of water, such as rivers and oceans, eroding the ground.

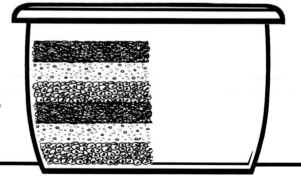

3. First, experiment with what happens with ocean wave erosion. This is the type of erosion Mary Anning dealt with at Lyme Regis. Carefully pour water into the empty half of your tub. Notice what happens as soon as the water is added.

4. Now simulate waves beating against the shore by moving the water with your hands. What happens to your hill? Sedimentary rocks are soft and erode easily. Towns like Lyme Regis have to build seawalls to protect the land and prevent homes and buildings from falling into the ocean.

5. Rain can also erode sedimentary hills. To demonstrate this, build another hill on one side of your second tub. Layer the gravel, sand, and soil just like you did earlier. Make sure to pack it tightly.

6. This time, use a watering can to simulate rain. Pour water from the can onto the top of the hill. What happens to the soil, sand, and rocks? Imagine how a storm with strong ocean waves would affect sedimentary cliffs like those at Lyme Regis. New fossils would be exposed from the erosion, but the hills would be unstable.

2

Discovery of Dinosaurs

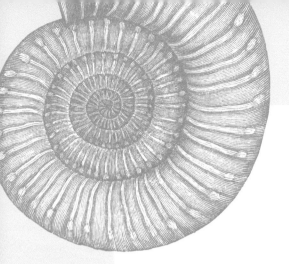

The weeks after Richard's death were painful for the whole family. They missed his booming laugh and his excitement at each discovery. They missed his hammering and building in his workshop, and they missed the income he brought to the family. Without Richard the family was destitute.

Molly had to apply to the local church for help. In those days there was no welfare, no life insurance, and no way for widows and orphans to get help except through charitable organizations like the church. The Annings were awarded a small monthly allowance that was barely enough to buy bread. But at least they had something to eat.

Molly decided 14-year-old Joseph had to go to work. He was apprenticed to a local upholstery maker. He didn't receive any income, but he learned a trade that provided him with a career path, and he was given meals. It was one less mouth to feed at home.

Mary was left doing what she hated most, which was housework. Her mother suffered from depression after Richard's death and left most of the chores to Mary. To make a little money, Mary also cleaned and ran errands for a few of the wealthier people in the neighborhood. With her brother away at his job and her mother quiet and

sad, Mary was often alone. The only time she felt happy was when she could sneak away to the shore to hunt for a few fossils and remember better days.

A Glimmer of Hope

On one of these outings, Mary found a particularly beautiful ammonite. As she was carrying home her treasure, she met a tourist hunting fossils on the beach. The young woman exclaimed over Mary's find and offered to buy it from Mary for a half crown. A half crown was a fortune to Mary. It was enough money to keep the Annings in food for weeks.

Mary quickly agreed and ran home to proudly hand over her fortune. It was then that Mary realized her father's business did not have to die with him. Mary would become the fossil hunter.

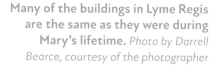

Many of the buildings in Lyme Regis are the same as they were during Mary's lifetime. *Photo by Darrell Bearce, courtesy of the photographer*

Someday she might even have her own shop with a glass front window. It had been Father's dream. Now it was hers.

Molly reluctantly agreed to allow Mary to return to the hills and shore she loved so much. If she was successful, it would save the family from near starvation. It certainly paid more than maid work or the fish market.

Mary was thrilled to be back in the world she loved. Out early in the morning, with her wild dark hair pulled back in a bun and hat tied onto her head, she became a familiar figure to the towns-people. She wore sturdy shoes and skirts that were often caked with mud. With her ever-trusty collection bag slung over her shoulder and her pick at the ready, she was always on the lookout for a good find. Being on the shore brought back good memories and provided new adventures.

Some days she was joined by her fossil-hunting friends the Philpot sisters. The Philpots had been a part of Mary's life since she was a six-year-old, scrambling up the cliffs with her father. Elizabeth Philpot was especially close to Mary, even though she was 10 years older and came from a wealthy family. The two often compared fossils and discussed their theories about the strange rocks and bones.

On other days, Mary was alone climbing the slippery, ocean-washed rocks and scouring the ground for fossil treasures. Mary not only missed her father, but she also missed her brother's companionship.

Joseph didn't have much time for fossil hunting, but when he could get away from his

apprenticeship, he eagerly joined his sister in the hunt. Together they were a formidable team. They could spot the shiny glint of a bone protruding from the clay when another person would have never noticed a thing. Their eyes were trained to see differences in the rock and recognize bone, shell, and tooth patterns.

A Fantastic Find

One winter afternoon in 1811, Joseph spotted part of a skull. With Mary's help, they dug out a strange head that had a long snout like a crocodile

Build a Rock Collection

Mary and Joseph Anning began collecting rocks and fossils when they were small children. Gathering rocks from the hills and beaches near their home helped them learn to identify different rocks and minerals and gave them an understanding of the layers of rocks where fossils could be found.

You can build a rock collection and practice organizing and recording specimens the way Mary Anning did.

MATERIALS

- Bags for collecting
- Journal (see page 27)
- Pen or pencil
- Soft toothbrush
- White acrylic paint (found in craft stores)
- Fine-tipped paintbrush
- Permanent marker
- Compartmentalized box—plastic craft boxes, egg cartons, and fishing tackle boxes work well
- Rock and mineral field guide from the library or a bookstore

1. First, you need to gather some specimens. Head outside to locate rocks for your collection, bringing along a bag to put them in. Try to find samples that have different colors and textures. Collecting rocks can be as simple as searching in a park or yard near you.

2. Keep track of where you found the rocks by recording them in a journal. Be sure to observe if the rocks you find are in their natural state (buried in soil or protruding from a **road cut**) or if they have been hauled in from another location (landscape rocks or road gravel).

3. If you are collecting at more than one site in a day, be sure to label your bags with the locations of where you collected the rocks. This will make it easier when you get home with your rocks and are ready to label them.

4. At the end of each collecting session, take time to clean your rocks. Do this by running them under water and gently scrubbing them with a soft toothbrush. Be careful—some specimens may be fragile! Let the rocks dry thoroughly.

5. Label each rock with a specimen number. First, paint a small circle of white paint on the rock, then allow it to dry. Then use a marker to write a number in the center of the paint dot.

6. Record the number of each rock sample in your journal along with the location of where you found it. Place it in a

compartmentalized box that will serve as your collection box and store it in a dry place. Water is the enemy of rock collections and can ruin your specimens.

7. Use a rock and mineral field guide to identify your rocks. You can check one out at the library or purchase one at a bookstore. You can also use the Hardness Test, Streak Test, and Cleavage Tests explained in this book (page 77) to assist in identification.

8. Make sure you update your records each time you collect new samples. Record keeping is essential for good science.

and huge eye sockets. This was a treasure they could sell! But Mary and Joseph also knew that there was a possibility that the rest of the animal's bones might be buried somewhere on the hillside.

The siblings decided to store the skull in the workshop and keep their eyes open for more bones that might match the skull. If they could find a whole crocodile, they could demand a higher price. When Joseph returned to his upholstery job, Mary promised to keep looking.

For months she didn't see any crocodile bones. There were fossilized shells, bits of fossil wood, and pieces of bone, but not a crocodile body. Then one day when the sea washed away a new section of the cliff, Mary saw glints of bone in the clay. She scaled the hill and picked away at the rock and mud. She chipped out several vertebrae. Could these belong to the crocodile head?

Mary kept digging. She kept finding more bones. How big was this animal? The more she dug, the more bones she found. And they didn't look like bones that belonged to a crocodile. The

Ichthyosaurus head discovered by Joseph and Mary Anning. The body has been lost. *Photo by Darrell Bearce, courtesy of the British Natural History Museum*

neck was too long, and Mary couldn't find any feet. Instead, some bones looked like they belonged to the flipper of a dolphin. This was one strange fish. But there were animals deep in the ocean that Mary had never seen. Maybe this was one of them. And maybe this was a treasure that would provide much-needed money.

Mary spent many days digging out bones, but there were still more locked in the cliff. She knew time was not in her favor. Any day another storm or landslide might wash her precious fossils out to sea. She needed help. Fortunately, several mine-workers in town were willing to assist with the dig. They were experienced, understood how the rocks would break along their grain, and were able to extract the fossils in large slabs. Mary offered to pay them from the meager money she had earned from the sale of other fossils. The men were probably willing to help the young girl because they had known her father and understood the family depended on income from the fossils to survive.

With the men's assistance, Mary collected all the bone pieces and brought them back to her father's old workshop. There she began the painstaking process of cleaning and sorting. Most of the bones were encased in shale.

To get a good price, Mary had to remove as much shale as possible without damaging the fossils. It took hours of work, scraping delicately at the shale, removing it bit by bit. If she was lucky, the shale crumbled into dust, filling the workshop with a layer of gray grit. When she was unlucky, the shale stuck hard, and Mary chipped with a chisel and prayed she didn't crack the bones.

After weeks of work, the fossils were clean and ready to assemble. When Mary laid out the bones, the animal was 17 feet (5 m) long. The head did resemble a crocodile but with much larger eye sockets. The neck was longer than a crocodile's, and instead of feet, the animal had flippers and a long tail. It was something Mary had never seen before. Maybe it was something no one had seen before.

Word spread quickly around the village of Lyme Regis and eventually reached the ears of a local wealthy landowner, Henry Hoste Henley. He bought the strange, fossilized animal for the London Museum and paid Mary 23 pounds. It was enough money to pay the rent and buy food for several months. Mary and her mother were thrilled. But the world of scholars and museum scientists was shocked at the strange discovery.

The Fossil That Rocked the World

The fossilized skeleton Mary uncovered matched none of the living animals known to science. Some scientists argued it was proof some animals had lived on Earth long before humans, and the animals had gone extinct. This went against the teachings of the Bible that the world was created in six days. Another common interpretation at the time was that everything created was still alive. This was a very old idea called "the Great Chain of Being." People who subscribed to this theory argued that the type of animal Mary discovered was still alive. It was simply hidden somewhere

ICHTHYOSAURS IN THE WILD

The *Ichthyosaurus* was in fact an extinct predator that glided hungrily through the Jurassic seas nearly 180 million years ago. Its long, flexible body moved quickly through the water, chasing after prehistoric squid and smaller marine animals, reaching cruising speeds of over 25 miles per hour (40 kmph).

While they probably looked like modern tuna or dolphins, they were not fish nor mammals; they were reptiles. *Ichthyosaur* means "fish lizard." The earliest ichthyosaurs did not have paddles and probably swam like undulating eels. But as they changed and adapted, ichthyosaurs developed paddles and fins with movements similar to modern fish. Ichthyosaurs didn't have gills as fish do and instead had lungs. They had to take oxygen from the air like modern whales, probably surfacing their nostrils to breathe.

Paleontologists know that ichthyosaurs did not lay eggs but instead gave birth to well-developed babies. Rare fossils have been discovered that show a mother ichthyosaur giving birth to multiple babies, with fossilized litters found to have as many as 11 embryos.

Scientists believe ichthyosaurs swam in pods or schools like today's tuna and dolphins, helping each other hunt. They had to be on the watch for the aggressive **mosasaurs** that enjoyed having ichthyosaurs for supper.

Illustration of living ichthyosaurs.
Nobu Tamura, courtesy of the artist, Wikimedia Commons, https://en.m.wikipedia .org/wiki/File:Ichthyosaurus_anningae_trio _NT_small.jpg

Paleontologists are still learning about this fascinating ancient marine lizard. Remains of three different types of ichthyosaurs were discovered in the Swiss Alps at an astonishing altitude of 9,200 feet (2,800 meters). Remains from one of the animals show that this *Ichthyosaurus* would have been 65 feet (20 m) long and weighed 80 tons (73 metric tons). That's a dinosaur as long as a bowling alley and as heavy as a locomotive engine. How did this monster of a fish lizard end up in the Alps?

Geologists believe that 180 million years ago, ichthyosaur bones were preserved on the floor of the ancient ocean that once covered Switzerland. Then 20 million years ago, shifting **plate tectonics** caused the continents to collide, pushing the ocean layer up and forming mountains. The fossils of the ichthyosaurs and other prehistoric animals traveled with the rock.

Scientists wonder how many other fossilized animals are hidden under the rocks and snow of mountain ranges. Could they discover a totally new type of dinosaur? Only time and research will tell.

Ocean Fossil Formation

During the **Mesozoic Era**, the Earth was much warmer. Tropical areas with forests and swamps covered much of the land. As plants and animals died, their bodies traveled from the swamps into the oceans along with sand and silt, piling up layers of organic materials on the seafloor. These layers were covered with more mud, sand, and silt, which blocked out air, and the organic material did not rot. Instead, the pressure of the increasing layers of mud preserved the organic material and created fossils.

You can simulate this process to understand how ocean fossils are formed.

MATERIALS

- Paper towels
- 1 slice of white bread
- Gummy fish or worms
- 1 slice of rye bread
- 1 slice of wheat bread
- Stack of heavy books

1. Lay a sheet of paper towel on the table and place the white bread on the paper. The bread represents the ocean floor.

2. Next, lay some gummy fish or worms on the ocean floor. They represent animals that died whose bodies sank.

3. Place a slice of rye bread on top of the gummies. This slice represents the layer of soil and sediments that travel from the swamps into the oceans.

4. Put another layer of gummy fish or worms on top of the sediment layer. These are animals who died whose bodies washed into the sea.

5. Place the slice of wheat bread on top. This represents additional sediments that have washed into the ocean over millions of years.

6. As the layers of sediment build up, so does the pressure. Place a paper towel on top of the last slice of bread, then place the stack of books on the bread stack. This simulates the pressure from layers of sediments and the ocean.

7. Leave your experiment like this for 48 hours to simulate millions of years.

8. After two days have passed, your experiment is ready for you to examine. Remove the books and notice how the pressure has compressed the layers. What does this tell you about what happens to soil and sediments over millions of years?

9. Now try to remove the layers and find the "fossilized" worms and fish. Notice the impressions they made on the layers of bread. These represent cast models. Is it difficult to remove the gummies from the bread? Or is it easy? How hard would it be for paleontologists to remove their fossils from layers of soil and rock?

that people had not explored, like the deepest jungles, remote islands, or the middle of the ocean. Religious leaders doubted that anything God made could stop existing. The idea of animals going extinct seemed blasphemous.

The concept of extinction was embraced by fossil hunters like William Buckland and Georges Cuvier. They speculated that the bones buried in rock were animals that lived millions of years before humans. Astonishing animals that looked like huge monster lizards had roamed the Earth and swum in the oceans.

Priests and preachers said these animals were not documented in the Bible and accused the scientists of heresy, or fighting against the church. Scientists argued with the priests. Scientists argued with other scientists. Mary Anning's fossils were part of a huge controversy that raged as people tried to understand the extraordinary signs of earlier life being discovered around the world.

Up and down the coast of Dorset County, where Lyme Regis was located, fossil hunters like Mary were digging up new specimens, and scientists were eager to add them to their collections. By the time she was a teenager, Mary had a full-time job collecting and **articulating** fossil skeletons. Her mother acted as her sales agent, writing letters to wealthy collectors, offering the newest specimens for sale. Joseph helped search for fossils when he had time off from his apprenticeship. The Annings were still poor, but Mary's work helped keep them fed and housed.

COMPANIONSHIP FOR MARY

Mary's life was often lonely. She spent most of her time alone either hunting for specimens or cleaning and preparing them in her workshop. Joseph was busy learning the upholstery trade and eventually married and had his own family. He occasionally went fossil hunting with Mary, but he had his own responsibilities.

Mary's mother lived with her all her life and helped in the shop but didn't go on field expeditions to collect fossils. That was Mary's job. Most days Mary probably enjoyed being outside, following her intuition, and being her boss. But sometimes it probably would have been nice to have a companion to share the work.

It is no surprise that Mary welcomed the companionship of a lively little dog she named Tray. Every morning, no matter what the weather, Tray was ready to follow Mary across the rocks, through the mud, and even into the ocean. The little dog sniffed for critters and chased the waves as Mary worked.

Stories have been told about Tray and how loyal he was to Mary. The townspeople knew that if Tray was wandering the hills or beaches, Mary was at work hunting fossils. People claimed that Mary trained Tray to sit, stay, and guard any fossils that she found. If Mary needed to go back for tools, Tray waited by the fossil until Mary returned.

Tray was a loyal companion until the moment of his death. In 1833 he and Mary were fossil hunting when rocks shifted and crashed down the hill. Mary barely escaped, and poor Tray was killed by the landslide. Mary's heart was broken. She wrote of her sadness to her friend Charlotte Murchison, explaining that the death of her faithful dog had "quite upset" her.

Mary never had another companion quite like Tray and missed the little dog for the rest of her life.

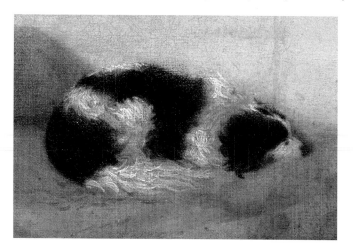

The only known image of Tray, from a painting of Mary Anning (see page 36). *Courtesy of Wikimedia Commons*

Bone Extraction

One of the most difficult jobs for a paleontologist is extracting and cleaning a fossil. Most fossils are encased in stone, and it takes a great deal of skill and practice to know how to remove the excess rock without damaging the fossil. Mary Anning was highly respected for her ability to clean and repair fossils.

You can do an experiment to learn how difficult it is for paleontologists to prepare specimens for display.

MATERIALS

- Dried chicken bones (or other small bones)
- Safety goggles
- Nitrile gloves (plaster of Paris can be hard on the skin, drying it out quickly.)
- Plaster of Paris mix
- Water
- Aluminum foil pie pan
- An assortment of tools: small picks or awls, small hammer, screwdriver, old toothbrush, tweezers

1. The next time your family has chicken for supper, ask an adult to save some of the bones for you. Make sure the bones are washed and cleaned of all meat. Set the bones out to dry for at least a week, in a place where no pet or animal can get to them. When the bones are dry and no longer oily, you are ready to begin the experiment.

2. Wearing safety goggles and nitrile gloves, mix plaster of Paris with water according to the directions on the package. You will need enough to fill the pie pan to the top.

3. When you have filled the pan with plaster, place the bones in the wet plaster. Spread them around so they are not clumped in one place.

4. Let the plaster fully harden. This usually takes over 24 hours.

5. Once the plaster is hard, remove it from the pie pan. Take this plaster "pie" outside for the excavation phase. It can get messy. **Make sure you wear safety goggles to protect your eyes, just like paleontologists do.**

6. Your job is to work just like a paleontologist does to remove the bones from the rock. You need to keep the bones from breaking and remove as much plaster as you can without damaging the specimen. You can use the tools you have collected to pry the bones from the plaster. This is exactly what scientists must do to remove fossil bones from rock.

7. Did you find it easy or difficult to remove the bones? Do you think it would be easier to extract large bones or small ones? What problems do you think scientists have when they try to extract fossils from rock?

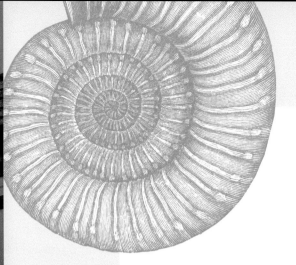

3

Professional Fossilist

Working as a full-time fossil hunter meant spending almost every day scouring the beaches along Lyme Regis, climbing the slippery cliffs, and cracking open small boulders. Some days Mary Anning found loose fossils or split open a stone to reveal a perfect ammonite. Other days she came home empty-handed. The biggest discoveries were often made after a violent storm when the rain and wind caused landslides. As the cliffs crumbled to the ground, they revealed fossilized bones, teeth, skulls, and vertebrae.

Cockamoile Square as it is today. The home where Mary lived as a child has been replaced with the Lyme Regis Museum. *Photo by Darrell Bearce, courtesy of the photographer*

Once she spotted a fossil, it was a race against the tide and waves threatening to drag the treasure out to sea. It was treacherous work, because the Blue Lias soil that made up the hills was slick as ice and sticky as quicksand when it was wet. And it was almost always wet. Mary often strapped small wooden platforms called *pattens* onto the bottoms of her shoes. They helped keep her shoes from being sucked into the muck.

To protect her head from falling rocks, she shellacked an old top hat to make it stiff and hard. She probably would have liked to wear pants like her brother and the other men, but that would have created a scandal. During Mary's lifetime, women were expected to wear long dresses. The skirts made climbing the cliffs even more dangerous for Mary, but they didn't stop her. She was always on the hunt for fossils by herself or with companions.

Friends in the Field

One of her fossil hunting friends was the wealthy Henry De la Beche. The son of a Jamaican sugar plantation owner, he and his mother moved to Lyme Regis in 1812 during the time Mary discovered the first ichthyosaur skeleton. Henry was 16, the same age as Mary's brother Joseph, and just three years older than Mary.

Many of the townspeople could not understand why the wealthy young man chose to traipse across the rocks and dig in the dirt with that unusual Anning girl. Mary was nothing like the young ladies people expected Henry to socialize with. Mary wore rugged clothing, was perpetually dirty, and had rough, weathered skin. She had no social graces and no financial resources.

Henry and Mary's friendship was based on their mutual interest in fossils and natural history. Scrambling up and down the hills, they spent hours debating the origin of the fossilized shells, bones, and teeth.

Because of Henry's wealth, he had access to scientific books and pamphlets. He shared his knowledge with Mary and loaned her papers and articles that she meticulously hand-copied to study later. Books were much too expensive for Mary to purchase, and there were no lending libraries. She depended on her wealthier friends to stay informed about new scientific discoveries and theories.

Mary became friends with many people in the scientific community, including William and Mary Buckland. They met when Mary was just 16 and William came to Lyme Regis to hunt fossils. William was a clergyman and a few years later was named the first reader (professor) in the new science of geology at Oxford University. His wife, Mary Morland, was a talented naturalist and illustrator. William was known as an eccentric scientist who took his pet bear to classes and served his dinner guests strange delicacies like mice on toast. He was always up for an adventure and eagerly

Make a Science Journal

For most of her life, Mary Anning collected science information and kept it in special notebooks so that she could better understand the animals she excavated and the world around her. She copied drawings, scientific papers, and quotes from people she admired. These journals helped her learn about discoveries and analyze her findings.

You can create a journal where you can record the specimens you find and save articles about important scientific breakthroughs.

MATERIALS

* Three-ring binder or spiral notebook
* Notebook paper
* Pencil
* Markers
* Stickers or magazine pictures
* Glue

1. You can use either a three-ring binder or a spiral notebook for your journal. The advantage of a three-ring binder is that it lets you easily add new pages and move papers around without tearing up your journal.

2. Decorate the cover of the journal to make it uniquely yours. Draw pictures of your favorite dinosaurs, fossils, rocks, or crystals. Create a collage of pictures from magazines or embellish the cover with stickers.

3. Now you're ready to fill up your journal. There are tons of great sites on the Internet about fossils and prehistoric animals. Several are listed in the Resources section at the end of this book (page 114). You can copy the information by hand as Mary Anning did, or you can use modern technology and print out articles and glue them into your journal.

4. Keep a section of the journal for recording your nature and rock experiences. When you are outside, study the animals, plants, and stones around you. Write and draw your observations. These investigations will help you become an astute scientist, just like Mary Anning.

followed Mary down the cliffs and into the sea in search of fossils. Unlike some of his fellow clergy, William had no difficulty with the idea of extinct animals, believing there was room for a broader interpretation of the biblical timeline of creation.

The Bucklands became lifelong friends of Mary's. Over the years they exchanged ideas and letters, conducted scientific experiments, and uncovered new dinosaur bones. Mary may not have had much formal schooling, but her mind was stretched and shaped by the scientists she worked with. She devoured new facts and developed her understanding and theories of prehistoric life.

The cliffs of Lyme Regis were good to Mary, and for the next few years, she was able to make a living selling partial skeletons, ichthyosaur skulls, teeth, and large ammonites to the scientific community and amateur fossil collectors. She also earned money taking visiting professors on outings and teaching them how to locate specimens hidden in the mud.

When she was 19, Mary discovered another amazing ichthyosaur skeleton. This one included all four of the animal's paddle-like limbs and was quickly purchased by fossil enthusiast Lieutenant Colonel Thomas Birch. Unfortunately, that was the last large fossil Mary found for several months. The smaller ammonite and belemnite fossils sold during the tourist season didn't provide enough income. Selling larger skeletons to wealthy collectors and museums was how Mary paid the bills. But as hard as Mary searched, the hills refused to release their treasures. Even storms did not uncover any large skeletons.

Some Help from Friends

A year later, when Colonel Birch visited, the Annings were so desperate for money they were selling their furniture to pay the rent. Colonel Birch was shocked. He knew that many of the magnificent specimens on display in museums and private collections had been discovered, excavated, and meticulously prepared by Mary Anning. He realized that Mary was not getting credit for her discoveries, nor was she being adequately compensated for her scientific work.

Somebody had to help, and Colonel Birch volunteered. He wrote in a letter to his friend Gideon Mantell:

The fact is that I am going to sell my collection for the benefit of the poor woman and her son and daughter at Lyme who have in truth found almost all the fine things which have been submitted to scientific investigations: when I went to Charmouth and Lyme last summer I found these people in considerable difficulty—on the act of selling their furniture to pay their rent— in consequence of their not having found one good fossil for near a twelvemonth. I may never again possess what I am about to part with; yet in doing it I shall have the satisfaction of knowing that the money will be well applied, the sale is to be at Bullock's in Piccadilly in the middle of April. Should you then be in town don't miss seeing it.

Colonel Birch's sale was a success and brought in over 400 pounds. The Anning family was deeply grateful for the colonel's generosity. The money enabled the family to stay in the fossil business, and it brought attention to Mary's talent for locating and excavating unusual specimens.

Days of Discovery

Local newspapers and monthly news magazines began reporting on her findings. In 1821 it was noted that:

Productive as the coast of Dorsetshire (between Charmouth and Lyme) has been in specimens of organised fossils, the interesting vestiges of the primaeval world, none have hitherto been discovered there of so fine a character, and in such rare perfection, as a skeleton found upon a ledge of rock, a few days since, by Miss Mary Aming [Anning], of Lyme, about half a mile to the eastward of that town. The animal, whose remains have been thus brought to light by this persevering and successful collector of extraneous fossils, appears to have been one of the species called Ichthyosaurus vulgaris, *which, in times we know nothing of, was a common inhabitant of the parts where his bones at present repose.*

It was while she was hunting for *Ichthyosaurus* skeletons that Mary found an odd set of bones. The vertebrae of this animal were longer than those of the ichthyosaur, and the bones of the paddles also looked completely different. The neck of the beast seemed to be at least twice as long as an *Ichthyosaurus.*

Mary's old friend Henry De la Beche and fellow scientist William Conybeare were sure this was an entirely new type of animal. They were so confident they even named the animal before they found a complete skeleton. The mystery creature was dubbed a plesiosaur.

Mary and Henry spent the next two years searching for a body to go with the name. During that time Mary excavated four more *Ichthyosaurus* skeletons and sold them to customers like the British Museum and patrons of the Bristol Institution for the Advancement of Science. She also found more signs of the elusive *Plesiosaurus,* collecting additional vertebrae, bones from paddles, and pieces of ribs. But by November 1823, she still had not found a full skeleton, and Henry had to leave to visit his Jamaican plantations. Mary kept searching as Henry traveled.

A storm roared through Lyme Regis on the night of December 9, 1823. Massive waves crashed against the seawall and battered the cliffs. The next morning Mary headed out, anxious to see if the storm had washed out any new fossils. Fresh layers of mud, shale, and limestone were piled on the beach. Mary scanned the debris with her experienced eye. A piece of bone glinted in the gray light. She dug through the sticky gray muck carefully, extracting her treasure.

It was a skull. But this was not the big-eyed, long-snouted skull of an *Ichthyosaurus.* This skull was small with a snub nose and little eye sockets. Could this be the head of the animal Henry had named *Plesiosaurus*? If it was, there would be vertebrae and other bones close to it.

DURIA ANTIQUIOR

Henry De la Beche was fascinated with the ancient creatures Mary excavated. He was present when Mary's first *Ichthyosaurus* was pulled out of the Lyme Regis hills and had been the one to urge Mary to look for the bones of the *Plesiosaurus*.

A collector himself, Henry liked to imagine what life was like when England was covered with ocean and the giant reptiles ruled the sea. What did the animals look like? Was their skin scaly or smooth? Were they the same color as modern reptiles? How did they live? How did they fight?

In 1830 Henry painted *Duria Antiquior*, a watercolor depicting his idea of ancient Dorset, England. It was the first version of what is now known as *paleoart*. Paleoart is defined as any original artistic work that attempts to depict prehistoric life according to scientific evidence. Henry's picture shows a large ichthyosaur biting the neck of a plesiosaur while another plesiosaur is trying to scare a crocodile on the land. **Pterosaurs** are flitting across the sky while other ancient creatures battle it out in the water.

When he showed his painting to friends, it was met with resounding approval, and Henry decided to hire illustrator Georg Scharf to make professional prints known as *lithographs* based on his watercolor. The profit from sales of the lithographs would go to help his old friend Mary Anning and her family through financial difficulties.

The prints were so popular that Henry had to commission a second printing to keep up with demand. William Buckland kept a supply of the pictures on hand to display during his geology lectures. Copies of the print were purchased by scientists in France and Germany. Because of Henry's picture, other geologists began illustrating their books with pictures of ancient life based on fossil evidence.

Today museums and galleries often have art or dioramas that depict prehistoric life. But in 1830, this was a new concept, and it ignited the imaginations of generations of young scientists.

Duria Antiquior, painted in 1830 by the geologist Henry De la Beche based on fossils found by Mary Anning. *Courtesy of Wikimedia Commons*

Mary scraped and dug until she found what she was looking for. Sections of vertebrae locked into stone. So many pieces. She needed help getting them out before they were claimed by the waves. Mary took the skull and ran back to town. She hired workers, who helped her dig late into the night.

Quarrying out the skeleton was backbreaking work. Most of the bones were lodged in pieces of limestone. The heavy rocks had to be hauled from the beach up the steep hill to Mary's workshop, half a mile away. Some of the smaller pieces Mary lugged up the hill herself in her collecting bags. The largest stones were loaded onto either carts or the back of a hired donkey and moved to the Anning home.

A Different Kind of Dinosaur

As soon as she began cleaning the fossil, Mary realized the animal was unique. This had to be the plesiosaur. But Henry was hundreds of miles away missing the incredible discovery.

As she cleaned the bones and arranged them in order, Mary marveled at this ancient sea creature. It stretched nine feet (2.7 m) long and was six feet (1.8 m) wide with a tiny head only seven inches (17.8 cm) long. The neck was disproportionately long, making up two-thirds of the body. The whole frame consisted of nearly 90 vertebrae, and 35 of those were in the neck. Mary was astonished, especially when she compared this creature to modern long-necked animals. The giraffe had only seven neck vertebrae, and the ostrich had just nine.

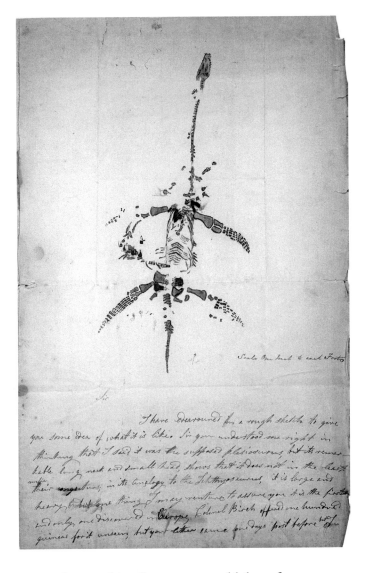

Plesiosaur drawing and letter by Mary Anning.
Courtesy of Wikimedia Commons

Realizing this discovery would be of great interest to her scientific clients, Mary drew a detailed sketch of the animal and sent letters to prospective customers. She received multiple offers and agreed to sell it to the Duke of Buckingham for 100 pounds. Mary's old friend William Buckland came as a representative of the duke to examine the fossil in person and complete the deal. William was amazed by the huge specimen and described it as follows:

PLESIOSAURS

Plesiosaurs must have been an incredible sight swimming in the Jurassic seas with their giraffe-like necks and huge, rounded bodies. Some of them grew to lengths of 49 feet (15 m). That's like a semi-trailer swimming through the ocean. Their strong jaws allowed them to crunch through the shells of cephalopods and eat bony fish. But life wasn't easy for the plesiosaur. They had to be wary of the sharks and mosasaurs hunting them as food.

Like whales, the plesiosaurs had lungs and needed to breathe air. They also gave birth to a single well-developed baby and took care of it like mother whales. Baby plesiosaurs may have stayed with their mothers for several months learning how to hunt and defend themselves.

Some plesiosaur skeletons have been found with stones in their stomachs. The stones are called *gastroliths* and probably helped them digest the hard-shelled cephalopods like ammonites and belemnites.

Plesiosaurs roamed oceans all over the world, and their skeletons have been found on every continent, including Antarctica. The heaviest fossilized *Plesiosaurus* in the world was discovered on an island in Antarctica. This specimen of *Plesiosaurus* weighed a whopping 15 tons (13.6 metric tons). That's as big as two tyrannosauruses.

To the head of a Lizard, it united the teeth of a Crocodile; a neck of enormous length, resembling the body of a serpent; a trunk and tail having the proportions of an ordinary quadruped, the ribs of a Chameleon, and the paddles of a Whale.

Not everyone in the scientific community was thrilled with Mary's new fossil. Famous French scientist Georges Cuvier was sure that Mary had created a hoax by attaching the head and neck of a sea serpent to the body of an ichthyosaur.

Mary was furious. This kind of accusation could ruin her reputation as a knowledgeable fossil dealer and destroy her business. But when experts examined the skeleton, they agreed that this was no fake, and even Georges Cuvier had to admit he had been mistaken.

Since Henry De La Beche was still in Jamaica, William Conybeare presented the information about the plesiosaur to the Geological Society of London. Even though Mary was the person who found the skeleton, excavated it, and articulated it, she received no credit for her work. This was true for almost all her finds. The person who purchased the fossil was given the credit of ownership by museums, and the scientists received credit for the talks they gave about Mary's discoveries. Many of the specimens in museums across Europe were excavated and prepared by Mary, but the only clue is the label that states it was found in the area of Lyme Regis.

Even if Mary would have been recognized for her discoveries, she would never have been permitted to present her findings to the Geological Society. In the early 1800s, women were not allowed to attend its meetings, much less become a member. England did not grant women the right to attend university until 1868 and took until 1878 to consent to award degrees to females.

The lack of recognition for her painstaking work and knowledge had to be frustrating. But Mary was a practical woman and knew that fossil hunting was the career that gave her independence and a means to support herself. Without the fossil business, Mary would have been relegated to working as a household servant, a fishmonger, or a farm laborer.

With fossil hunting, she became a businesswoman who, at the age of 27, was able to realize both her and her father's dreams. She left the small, cold house near the ocean and moved with her mother up the hill to Broad Street. The thatched roof building provided a warm living space for Mary and her mother and housed Mary's fossil store and workshop. The hand-painted sign above the door announced the opening of Mary's Fossil Depot, and fossil specimens were proudly displayed in the glass front window. Mary created her own success.

(top) **Plesiosaur excavated by Mary Anning and on display at the British Natural History Museum.**
Photo by Darrell Bearce, courtesy of the British Natural History Museum

(right) **British Natural History Museum, London, houses numerous specimens collected by Mary Anning.**
Photo by Darrell Bearce, courtesy of the British Natural History Museum

Scientific Illustration

In the days before photography was invented, scientific illustration was a crucial way to convey discoveries to other scientists and the public. The abilities of professional illustrators like Mary Morland Buckland were highly prized, but almost every researcher was expected to have adequate drawing skills to record their findings. Mary Anning understood the importance of scientific illustration and took great care to document her discoveries with hand-drawn pictures.

To learn how to illustrate, many people copied drawings. This was how Mary Anning learned to illustrate her specimens, and you can use the same method to become a science illustrator.

MATERIALS

- ✹ Sample pictures
- ✹ Drawing paper
- ✹ Drawing pencils
- ✹ Eraser
- ✹ Ink pens
- ✹ Lightbox (optional) or bright window
- ✹ Tape

Plesiosaur mother with her baby. © N. Tamura, courtesy of the artist, Wikimedia Commons, https://commons.wikimedia.org/wiki/File:Augustasaurus_BW.jpg

1. Becoming a good illustrator takes practice. Lots of it! You can begin by copying the sample illustrations included in this activity. You may also find your sources for scientific illustrations in old books or on the Internet.

2. To get a feel for illustrating you can first trace the picture. If you have a lightbox, you can use that to do the tracing. A bright window works just as well. Simply tape a copy of the illustration you've chosen to the window. Tape your blank drawing paper over it. You should be able to see to do a nice tracing.

3. As you are tracing, pay attention to how the picture was drawn. Notice the details

of the animal and how the artist has chosen to illustrate them. You can learn a great deal from studying other people's work.

4. After you have made a tracing, try drawing the same picture again, but this time simply look at the other picture as a guide. Don't worry if your picture doesn't look exactly like the one you are copying. You will get better with practice. Artists learn to use muscle memory when they draw just like athletes when they play sports. The more you practice, the better you will be.

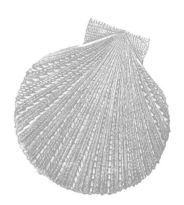

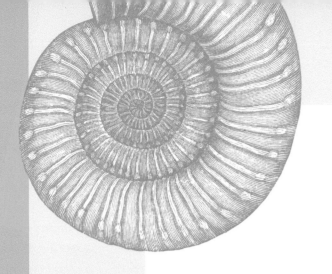

4

A Lasting Legacy

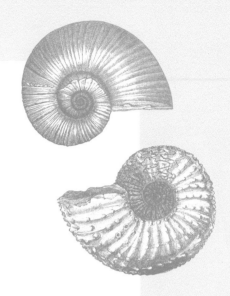

Mary Anning's Fossil Depot became a popular stop for Lyme Regis tourists. Ladies and gentlemen who wanted a souvenir of their seaside vacation purchased ammonites, belemnites, and crinoids just like they had when Anning's father was alive. But Anning's shop also catered to well-known scientists, wealthy fossil collectors, and even royalty.

When Frederick Augustus II, King of Saxony, visited Great Britain, he made a stop at Anning's shop. His companion, the naturalist Carl Gustave, wrote about the visit:

Portrait of Mary Anning and her dog, Tray. *Courtesy of Wikimedia Commons*

We fell in with a shop in which the most remarkable prettifications and fossil remains—the head of an Ichthyosaurus—beautiful ammonites, &c, were exhibited in the window. We entered and found the small shop and adjoining chamber completely filled with the fossil productions of the coast.

The king and his friend considered purchasing a six-foot-long *Ichthyosaurus* that had a very reasonable price of 15 pounds. They were eager to get the name of the shop owner so they might contact her.

I was anxious, at all events, to write down the address, and the woman who kept the shop—for it was a woman who had devoted herself to this scientific pursuit—with a firm hand, wrote her name, "Mary Annis," in my pocket-book, and added, as she returned the book into my hands, "I am well known throughout the whole of Europe."

Carl Gustave had obviously not heard of Anning, since he misread her last name. But Anning was not exaggerating about her fame. During her lifetime, her work and discoveries were frequently discussed at geological meetings from Paris to Switzerland to Berlin. She was also known in America because of the large specimens she sold to museums and collectors.

Small but Significant

But not all of Anning's discoveries were huge in size. One of her important breakthroughs came

from small cylindrical stones that were common on the beach. Locals called them *bezoar stones*, because they resembled the gallstones of bezoar goats. Anning found a good number of the stones in the abdomens and pelvises of the ichthyosaurs. Because of their spiral shape and rounded ends, Anning became convinced these were fossilized feces.

She consulted with her friend William Buckland, and together they began investigating. If this was fossilized animal dung, then it could contain the hard remains of the animal's food. Buckland and Anning spent hours crushing bezoar stones and found fossilized fish scales, tiny bones, small teeth, and pieces of shell—exactly like the feces of living animals.

Buckland renamed the bezoar stones **coprolites**. Scientists used them to learn more about the food sources and ecosystem of the ancient marine creatures. Coprolites are still studied today and give scientists information about everything from environmental conditions and animal diet to the types of fungus, spores, and plants that were abundant in each period of life on Earth.

Belemnites were another small fossil Anning collected. These narrow, long, conical stones were plentiful in a layer of rock called Black Ven and were the remains of an ancient cephalopod similar to a squid or cuttlefish. Anning often found small black-brown lumpy rocks scattered around the belemnites. They were of consistent size and shape.

Anning wondered if they might be ink sacs. Modern cuttlefish and squid squirt ink to scare away predators. Perhaps the ancient cephalopods did the same thing. William Buckland dissected a cuttlefish to compare and agreed that these strange stones were ink sacs. They found the ink could be reconstituted and used to write. He even sent some of the fossilized ink sacs to artist Sir Francis Chantrey, who used them to create drawings. Anning's friend and fellow fossil collector Elizabeth Philpot also experimented with creating pictures of fossils from fossilized ink.

In December 1828, Anning yanked a slab of limestone out of the cliffs and discovered a curious skeleton. Delicate bones lay embedded in the stone. The tangled mess contained two short legs, two birdlike feet, pieces of ribs, and two long arms, but no skull. At the end of each arm were four peculiar fingers. Three of the fingers were short but one was long and clawlike, similar to the arms of a bat.

Anning had read about fossils like this being found in Germany. They were flying reptiles named pterodactyls after the Greek words for "wing" and "finger." Anning's fossil was the first pterodactyl found in England.

William Buckland wrote about this incredible find in a paper for the Geological Society. When he presented his paper in 1829, he gave full credit to Anning for its discovery.

The winter wind and wild waves on the shores of Lyme Regis were bone-chillingly cold. But they also pounded away the eroding cliffs and often gave Anning some of her most unusual treasures. In December 1829, Anning spotted yet another unique skeleton. Only 19 inches (48 cm) long, the fossil possessed a large head with big eye sockets. The animal had a long, slim jaw with a frontal spine sticking out above it. The backbone was delicate and long with an amazing 260 vertebrae. Pressed into the limestone were faint impressions of elegant winglike fins.

Scientists were excited to examine the one-of-a-kind fossil and concluded it was a type of shark ray that had a skeleton made of cartilage. The scientists named the fossil *Squaloraja polyspondyla* and congratulated Anning on being the first person to find this amazing creature.

The London Adventure

While Anning's name was known in scientific circles, it did not translate into significant amounts of money or even popular fame. Anning worked

Illustration of *Pterodactylus* bones found by Mary Anning.
Courtesy of Wikimedia Commons

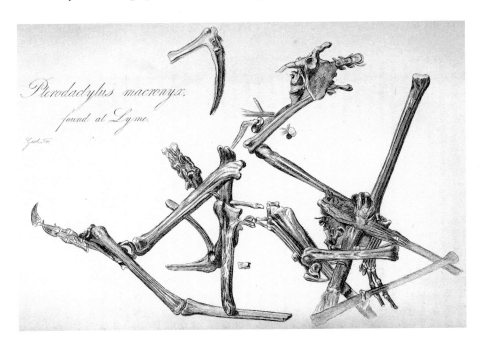

Pterodactylus macronyx.
found at Lyme.

hard all her life to keep her and her family barely above the poverty level. She never had the opportunity to travel like the scientists she worked with. Most of her life was spent in Dorset County near Lyme Regis. The biggest trip of her life came in 1829 when she traveled 154 miles (248 km) from Lyme Regis to the city of London.

Anning's friend and fellow fossil enthusiast Charlotte Murchison urged her to come to visit and see the sights of London. Anning had spent hours on the beaches with Murchison hunting for fossils. The two formed a close friendship despite the differences in their social standing. Society considered Murchison a proper lady. She was married to a husband who earned a good income and lived in a stylish part of London. Many people considered it improper for an upper-class woman like Murchison to be friends with the lower-class

PTEROSAUR

During the Mesozoic Era, the skies were filled with winged creatures. Whirling above the heads of apatosaurs and stegosaurs were the winged lizards called pterosaurs. Long before birds appeared on Earth, these animals dive-bombed into oceans, snatching up prehistoric fish for lunch and scooping up giant Mesozoic insects for snacks.

The first fossil evidence of a pterosaur was found in Germany in 1784 and described by naturalist Cosimo Alessandro Collini. He thought the strange fossil with a beak-like mouth and extremely long forelimbs was some sort of seagoing animal that used its front arms as paddles. But in 1800 Georges Cuvier examined a drawing of the fossil and realized that the long forelimbs were used as wings like a modern bat. He dubbed the animal Ptero-Dactyle. (The name was later changed to *Pterodactylus antiquus*.) It was the first known member of the incredibly diverse animal group now called pterosaurs.

When Mary Anning excavated her pterosaur in 1828, it was the first fossil of its kind found outside of Germany. During the next 50 years, there were partial bones of pterosaurs found but most were of very poor

Artist's rendition of the pterosaur known as **Hatzegopteryx.** *Mark Witton, courtesy of the artist, Wikimedia Commons, https://commons.wikimedia.org/wiki/File:Hatzegopteryx.png*

Anning. But their friendship flourished as they discussed science, fossils, and life. They kept in touch through letters, and Anning felt comfortable accepting the invitation to stay at Murchison's home.

London whirred with activity. Carriages clattered up and down streets teeming with people. Buildings rose four and five stories high, and churches had spires that reached the sky. Markets were crowded with people selling everything from fresh fish to bolts of beautiful fabric. It was a world completely different from the quiet coastal village of Lyme Regis.

Anning toured the British Museum, which housed an extensive collection of Egyptian sarcophagi, mummies, and burial relics, along with numerous Greek statues. In her journal, Anning noted that she enjoyed seeing the King's Library,

quality. Scientists realized that the lightweight hollow bones of the flying lizards could not stand up to the grinding pressure of rock and time, so very few specimens of the fossilized animal have been found.

Even though the fossils are rare, paleontologists have learned a great deal about these incredible creatures. There were two major types of pterosaurs. The *basal pterosaurs* had teeth and long tails, and their wing membranes were connected to their hind legs. Their anatomy would have made them awkward walkers, but they were probably good at climbing trees. The basal pterosaurs were relatively small, eating insects and other small **vertebrate** animals.

Later pterosaurs known as *pterodactyloids* had narrower wings that were not attached to the hind legs. Their tails were much smaller, and they were able to walk upright when they were on the ground. Some of them had huge head crests, and most had tough horny beaks.

Pterosaurs came in a wide variety of sizes. The smallest known pterosaur had a wingspan of 10 inches (25 cm) while the largest pterosaur was as tall as a giraffe and had a wingspan of 39 feet (11.9 m). That's the size of a four-seater airplane! This pterosaur is nicknamed Dracula because it was discovered in Romania. The neckbones of this animal are as wide as the body of a full-grown man.

Dracula the pterosaur is causing quite a debate among paleontologists. Some believe this gigantic animal was just too big to fly. Perhaps it was like an ostrich or emu and was flightless even though it had wings. Other paleontologists argue that the giant animal flew when it was younger and less heavy and became land-bound as it aged. It's one of the many mysteries that paleontology still has to solve.

Fizz Test— Locating Limestone

*Fossil hunters like Mary Anning need to know the right places to find fossils. Fossils are not usually found in **igneous rocks** that form deep inside the Earth. Digging on a granite cliff will not yield dinosaur bones. You need to find a good layer of limestone or shale for fossil hunting.*

Limestone is a sedimentary rock that is mainly made up of calcium carbonate. Layers of limestone were formed by deposits from seawater. This is why limestone often contains marine fossils. You can test rock specimens to see if they contain calcium carbonate with a simple Fizz Test.

MATERIALS

* Eyedropper
* Household vinegar
* Rock samples

1. Use the eyedropper to place 10 to 15 drops of vinegar on a rock sample.
2. Watch closely to see if the vinegar starts to bubble or fizz. This is a chemical reaction between the calcium carbonate in the rock and the acid in the vinegar.
3. If it fizzes, your rock is a variety of limestone or marble. If you locate layers of limestone or marble in roadcuts or hills, they are likely to contain fossils.

especially the prayer books of King Ethelbert, Lady Jane Grey, and King Henry VII. Religion was an important part of Anning's life, and while she was in London, she attended services with Murchison at the recently finished St. Mary's Church.

At the Geological Society's rooms in Somerset House, she was given a tour of the collections by curator William Lonsdale. The museum displayed a cast of her plesiosaur; the original had been sent to Paris. Anning was amazed at the accuracy of the casting and said she could "hardly distinguish the difference." It was an invigorating trip and gave Anning perspective on the importance of her work and discoveries.

Plesiosaurs

Back home in quiet Lyme Regis, Mary Anning eagerly returned to her cliffs and beaches to excavate new skulls, vertebrae, and coprolites. In December 1830 she found what she considered "the most beautiful fossil I have ever seen."

It was a juvenile plesiosaur embedded in shale. The head, neck, and body were all intact, as were three of the four paddles. Lord Cole, Earl of Enniskillen, purchased Anning's lovely specimen for 220 pounds. A paper written about the fossil by scientist Richard Owen gave credit to fossil owner Lord Cole and a collector named Thomas Hawkins, but never mentioned Mary Anning.

Thomas Hawkins was a thorn in Anning's side. A rich fossil collector, he could afford to hire teams of people to excavate a site, but he was not careful in his methods and often destroyed more

Engraving of the British Museum as it would have looked when Anning visited. *Courtesy of Wikimedia Commons*

than he recovered. He also liked his specimens to look perfect and would supplement his skeletons by reconstructing missing parts out of plaster and passing them off as real.

Anning believed it was important to science to examine the fossils as they were found and never added plaster parts to her skeletons, even though it would have helped her make more money.

One time when Thomas Hawkins was visiting Lyme Regis, Anning discovered a 5-foot-long (1.5 m) *Ichthyosaurus* skull. She knew that with a skull that size, the full skeleton would be enormous. Probably the largest skeleton she had ever found. But as Anning dug, she realized that the rest of the skeleton was buried too deep under the cliff. It was out of her reach.

Hawkins was excited by the skull and promptly purchased it from Anning, then set out to dig for the rest of the skeleton. Anning warned him that it was too deep under the rock, but Hawkins wouldn't listen. He hired a huge crew to dig out the bones. They shoveled and chiseled for two days and hauled away a huge section of the hill. But when they finally found the rest of the body and tried to move it, the bones shattered and crumbled.

That still didn't stop Hawkins. He solicited Anning's help and packed up all the bone fragments and shipped them to his home. There he reconstructed what he could from the bone pieces and filled the rest in with plaster. Anning was outraged. She labored to give her customers

Plan a Perfect Paleontological Trip

Mary Anning's trip to London allowed her to see a wide variety of plants, animals, and fossils. Her trip broadened her horizons and gave her a better understanding of the world around her.

You may not be able to visit London as Anning did, but you can plan a trip to a museum near you. Natural history museums have displays of fossils found in their local region as well as samples from around the world. Check with your family to see when you can make the trip.

To plan the perfect trip, you will need to set up a budget and make plans on how to cover the expenses, just as Anning did.

1. Find out the museum closest to you. You can use the Internet to search or find answers at your local library. Calculate how many miles (or kilometers) away it is and how much this will cost in fares on public transportation or in gasoline expenses.

2. Research the types of exhibits that are open for viewing. Make sure you check to see if there is an admission fee and if there are any special discounts.

3. Will this be a full-day trip? Will you need to include meals? Can you pack a lunch or is there someplace where you can buy food? Include this in your travel budget.

4. Once you have listed all the expenses and calculated a total, present your budget and plans to your family. If it is not in the budget right now, you can brainstorm ways to earn or save money for the trip.

5. If travel is not possible for you or your family, you can do the next best thing and go on a virtual visit to a museum. Here are a few links to wonderful online paleontological exhibits:

British Natural History Museum: *https://www.nhm.ac.uk/visit/virtual -museum.html*

Los Angeles County Natural History Museum: *https://nhm.org /stories/virtual-tour-dino-hall-english*

Museums of Western Colorado: *https://museumofwesternco.com /dinosaur-journey-virtual-tour/*

National Museums Liverpool: *https://www.liverpoolmuseums.org.uk /virtual-tours/dinosaurs-and-natural -world-virtual-tour*

Royal Tyrrell Museum: *https://tyrrellmuseum.com/learn /distance_learning/virtual_visit*

Smithsonian National Museum of Natural History: *https://naturalhistory .si.edu/visit/virtual-tour*

St. George Dinosaur Discovery Site: *https://utahdinosaurs.org/visit-the -museum/sgds-virtual-tour/*

scientifically accurate specimens. A forger like Hawkins could ruin the business and income of honest dealers like her.

Problems

Over the years, Mary Anning worked hard and saved as much money as she could. By the time she was 36, she had set aside 200 pounds. This was money she intended to invest to help her in old age when she would not be able to climb the cliffs and dig for fossils. Sadly, the man she trusted to do the investing died without giving Anning a receipt for her money. This meant she had no proof for her claim on the money. Once again, Anning and her mother found themselves in dire financial circumstances.

But Anning's friends rallied around her. Elizabeth Philpot led a community fundraising event, and William Buckland rallied the Geological Society. The members of the Geological Society agreed to provide Anning with an annual income of 25 pounds a year. It was about twice what a housemaid would earn and provided enough to keep Mary and her mother in food and shelter.

The small income was a relief for Anning. As more and more large fossils were uncovered by collectors around the world, the museums paid less for Anning's specimens. Sometimes they didn't want them at all. Still, Anning kept searching.

In 1840 the British Museum purchased three fossil starfish that Anning discovered and later bought a fossilized shark. Times were hard and got even worse when Anning's mother became ill. In October 1842, Molly Anning died. She was 79 years old. Her death was noted in the local newspaper.

Oct 5, at Lyme Regis, of paralysis. Aged 79, Mary, the widow of Richard Anning, and mother of the celebrated Miss Mary Anning the fossilist.

For the first time in her life, Mary Anning found herself living alone. She continued to search for fossils and run her shop, but the hard physical labor had taken its toll on her body. Anning felt weak and tired. When she consulted a physician, she learned she was suffering from breast cancer.

There were no treatments for cancer in the 1800s. The best the doctor could do was to give her some pain relief by prescribing laudanum. This was a drug made from the poppy plant and containing opium. In Anning's time, people used laudanum to treat everything from cardiac disease and cancer to headaches and cramps. It was even given to babies to help them sleep when they were teething. No one understood how addictive and dangerous the drug was.

As Anning's pain increased, it became impossible for her to continue collecting. Her old friend William Buckland came to the rescue and convinced the Geological Society to enlarge the amount of her annual payments in honor of her years of service to the scientific community. Anning's work and achievements were also recognized by the Dorset County Museum, and in July 1846 Anning was elected as its first honorary member.

Eight short months later, on March 9, 1847, Mary Anning died. She was buried in St. Michael's churchyard above the cliffs where she discovered so many of her fossils.

A Life Well Lived

Friends and colleagues from Great Britain and Europe mourned Anning's passing. Her childhood friend Henry De la Beche had become Sir Henry, director of the Geological Survey and president of the Paleontographical Society. He wrote an eloquent obituary praising Anning and her talents and delivered it to members of the Geological Society.

There are those among us in this room who know well how to appreciate the skill she employed

(from her knowledge of the various works as they appeared on the subject,) in developing the remains of the many fine skeletons of Ichthyosauri and Plesiosauri, which without her care would never have presented to comparative anatomists in the uninjured form so desirable for their examinations.

The church Anning attended for many years installed and dedicated a new stained-glass window in Anning's memory. The scenes in the window depict the six acts of mercy from St. Matthew's Gospel. The inscription at the base of the window reads:

This window is sacred to the memory of Mary Anning of this parish who died 9 March 1847 A.D. and is erected by the vicar of Lyme and

(left) **Mary and Joseph Anning's gravestone in Lyme Regis.**
Photo by Darrell Bearce, courtesy of the photographer

(right) **Plaque marking the site of Mary Anning's death. The home where she had her Fossil Depot has been destroyed.**
Photo by Darrell Bearce, courtesy of the photographer

The window still shines in the St. Michael Church and reminds all who see it of the remarkable woman who changed science with her discoveries.

Because Anning was a woman and not a member of the Geological Society, her papers were not preserved for history. Anning's nephew sold most of her notebooks, correspondence, and drawings to her old customer, the Earl of Enniskillen. The Earl gave them to geologist Richard Owen at the British Museum, but instead of receiving special attention, the papers were mixed in with other files and documents. Today only a few of Anning's drawings and writings remain. Some of them are housed in the archives at the British Natural History Museum and are available for scholars and researchers to review.

Fossils collected and prepared by Anning can also be seen at the British Natural History Museum. The first ichthyosaur skull discovered by Joseph and Mary is on display, but the body Mary worked so hard to uncover has been lost to history.

The museum has about 30 specimens that they can directly attribute to Anning. There are probably more, but as with all museums in the 1800s, the person who donated the fossils received credit on the displays and in the museum records. Other museums that house Anning's fossils include the

Window dedicated to Mary Anning inside the St. Michael Church.
Photo by Darrell Bearce, courtesy of the photographer

Oxford University Museum of Natural History, the Sedgwick Museum in Cambridge, and the Muséum national d'Histoire naturelle in Paris.

Anning's story was kept alive in tour books, scientific papers, and even in children's magazines. In 1865 the weekly magazine *All the Year*

Round published a story titled "Mary Anning, the Fossil Finder." In 1869 a new version of the story was published in the magazine *Chatterbox* along with an engraving of young Mary Anning finding fossils with her father.

Scientists honored Anning by naming several fossils after her. There is a fossilized coral named *Tricycloseris anningi*, a fossilized shell named *Anningella*, and a fossil crustacean called *Cytherelloidea anningi*.

One of the larger animals named after Anning was discovered in 1927 by Robert Broom. When he presented the mammal-like reptile he stated:

I propose to call it Anningia megalops in honour of Miss Mary Anning, of Lyme Regis. Though many of the finest specimens of fossil reptiles in the British Museum were discovered by Miss Anning, and these specimens formed the basis of much of the work of Home, Conybeare, De la Beche, Hawkins, and Owen, and thus helped to give Britain its high position in the history of vertebrate paleontology, I have long felt that the part played by Miss Anning has not been fully appreciated as one of the world's greatest fossil hunters and as a pioneer. Although it is about a hundred years since she

Interior of the Lyme Regis Museum.
Photo by Darrell Bearce, courtesy of the Lyme Regis Museum

did most of her work, one may perhaps still be allowed to lay a stone on the cairn of this most remarkable woman.

Anning's memory is honored in the Lyme Regis Museum, completed in 1901. It is a happy coincidence that the museum was built on the site of Anning's childhood home. No one realized Anning's house had been in that location until 1985 when the museum acquired an 1824 map of the area and researchers realized that the museum was constructed on part of the footprint of Anning's old home. Now, an entire museum section is proudly devoted to this hometown hero.

Today the Paleontological Association presents the Mary Anning Award in recognition of outstanding contributions to paleontology made by amateurs. In 2010 the Royal Society named Anning one of the most influential women in the history of British science.

Exterior of the Lyme Regis Museum, built on the site of Mary Anning's childhood home.
Photo by Darrell Bearce, courtesy of the photographer

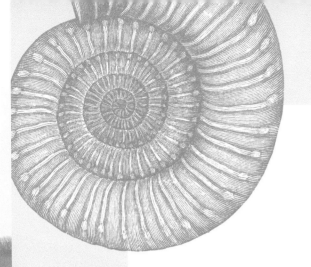

5

William and Mary Buckland

The summer wind whipped at the ocean waves splashing water in William Buckland's face. Laughing and wiping the spatter away, he waded deeper into the ocean. A perfect ammonite was rolling out with the waves—a quick grab and it would be his! William reached out an experienced hand, snatched the fossil from the sea, and dropped it in his sack. One more gorgeous specimen for his collection.

Village and beach of Lyme Regis, England. *Photo by Darrell Bearce, courtesy of the photographer*

William was a familiar sight on the beaches of Lyme Regis. Summer days found the Oxford professor with pants rolled up to his knees darting in and out of the waves, plucking up belemnites, crinoids, and fossil bones with his wife, Mary Moreland, and friend Mary Anning. He led his children on hikes and fossil hunting trips up and down the cliffs, regaling them with stories of the bizarre sea creatures that once ruled the ancient ocean. Most people thought he was just another vacationer escaping from the city, but William was one of the most famous geologists of his time. His ideas and discoveries helped create the science of paleontology.

Portrait of William Buckland.
Courtesy of Wikimedia Commons

William Buckland was born on March 12, 1784, in Axminster, England, less than seven miles from Lyme Regis. He spent his early childhood being homeschooled by his father, Trusham Charles Buckland, who served as the rector, or pastor, in charge of the Anglican church in Templeton. Fascinated by modern road improvements and mining, William's father often took him on hikes to investigate the new construction methods. The piles of rocks left behind were what interested William. He stuffed his pockets full of fossil shells, brachiopods, crinoids, and bits of fossilized wood.

Nature captivated Buckland. He collected birds' nests, feathers, bones, turtles, lizards, and rocks of all kinds. Hours were spent observing wriggling fish and slithering snakes. By the time he went to boarding school at Winchester College, Buckland was a devoted naturalist. Bright and eager to learn, he won a scholarship to Corpus Christi College in Oxford, where he studied for his bachelor's degree. His coursework involved classes in ancient languages, theology, and literature, but that wasn't enough for Buckland. He spent his free time in more lectures, learning human and animal anatomy in dissection classes, and attending lectures in geology, mineralogy, and chemistry.

On weekends, he tromped through the hills with the geology professor gathering specimens for his collection. In the summer Buckland mounted a horse and rode for miles exploring **caves**, road cuts, and eroding cliffs. He noted the different layers of rocks and created a geological **strata map** to help scientists understand the layers of the earth along the western coast of England.

Graduating with his master of arts degree in 1808, he was ordained as an Anglican priest in 1809 and named a fellow, or professor, of Corpus Christi College. In 1813 Buckland's expertise with rocks, minerals, and fossils was recognized when he was appointed the official reader in mineralogy at Oxford. Five years later he became Oxford's first reader in geology.

New Fossils, New Ideas

Buckland became one of the most popular speakers at the college. Students crowded into the lecture hall partly because Buckland's stories about ancient animals were intriguing and partly because they never knew what to expect. While most professors gave solemn traditional talks, Buckland stomped around on stage like a dinosaur. He brought in huge bones and jaws of extinct animals and sometimes even told jokes.

Students and friends who visited Buckland's rooms at Oxford found themselves in a maze of shelves stacked high with a jumbled mess of bones, skins, animal skulls, taxidermied animals, crystals, rock samples, and all manner of fossils. Every surface was covered by collections or books, leaving visitors nowhere to sit and very little room to stand. But visitors weren't there to be comfortable; they came to debate new theories about the age of the Earth and discuss the extraordinary bones being discovered.

As a priest, Buckland felt the need to reconcile the biblical view of creation being completed in six days with the scientific evidence of the Earth being millions of years old. Like many scientists of his time, Buckland subscribed to the Gap Theory, which posited there was a gap of time between two distinct creation stories in the first and second chapters of the book of Genesis. Gap Theorists believed that the universe was created eons ago, with plants and animals living for millions of years, but that the creation became evil and God destroyed it in a worldwide catastrophe, then re-created it in the familiar six-day story.

But some of Buckland's discoveries challenged this theory. As he traveled across Europe meeting with other scientists and exploring different **topographies** and fossils, he came to believe that there may have been a long series of mass extinctions and new creations. Some scientists believed the Great Flood described in the Bible might have been one of those catastrophes. Buckland believed there had been a flood but that it had not covered the entire Earth. He was able to examine this theory with the discovery of Kirkdale Cave in Yorkshire, England.

In the summer of 1821, workers in Yorkshire began to quarry limestone in a small cave. They noticed the floor of the cave was covered in bones but thought that they were probably the bones of cattle. Perhaps the cattle had died of an illness and a farmer had disposed of the bodies. The quarry workers shoveled out the bones and used them to repair the roads. The bones were quickly discovered by amateur geologists, who recognized them as prehistoric fossils.

Samples of the fossils were sent to Buckland at Oxford, and he identified a variety of bones, from

Cartoon drawn by William Conybeare showing William Buckland poking his head into a prehistoric hyena den. *Courtesy of Look and Learn, https://www.lookandlearn.com/history-images/YW068346L/Buckland-entering-the-Kirkdale-Cavern*

Kirkdale Cave. The light of his candle flickered off the bones and teeth of dozens of different animals. It was a treasure trove of ancient animal remains. Buckland was thrilled.

Back home Buckland analyzed the skeletons and found that while they were similar to living **species**, they were not the same. These bones came from animals that no longer roamed the Earth. The hyenas were a gigantic species that must have lived long ago. He visited zoos to watch how modern hyenas tore the meat from bones and the marks their teeth made. The patterns were consistent. The more he investigated, the more he was convinced that his theory was right.

In 1822 he wrote:

It must already appear probable, from the facts above described, particularly from the comminuted [pulverized] state and apparently gnawed condition of the bones, that the cave in Kirkdale was, during a long succession of years, inhabited as a den of hyaenas, and that they dragged into its recesses the other animal bodies whose remains are found mixed indiscriminately with their own: this conjecture is rendered almost certain by the discovery I made, of many small balls of the solid calcareous excrement [fossilized waste matter] of an animal that had fed on bones.

Scientists were impressed by Buckland's careful analysis and deductive reasoning. The Royal Society awarded him the Copley Medal for outstanding achievement in science. It was the equivalent of the modern-day Nobel Prize, and

elephants and rhinoceroses to hippopotamuses and giant hyenas. None of these animals had ever been seen in England. Some scientists argued that this was evidence of the Great Flood—that the animals had drowned and the bones washed into the cave.

Buckland didn't agree. He studied the bones and saw teeth marks on many of them. He came up with a different theory. What if the cave was a den for the hyenas? Maybe a time long ago, England had a different climate, and different animals wandered the woods and plains. Giant hyenas could have hunted elephants, hippos, and rhinos and dragged their bodies back to the cave to eat. If this was true, it could rock the worlds of both science and religion.

Buckland had to visit the cave.

On a cold December day in 1821, Buckland crawled through a slit in the earth and into the tiny

Cave Creation

William Buckland made important fossil discoveries by exploring the interior of caves. There he found the fossilized bones of prehistoric hyenas, rhinos, and hippos.

Caves can form through a chemical weathering process called dissolution. This happens when precipitation such as snowmelt and rain mix with carbon dioxide from the air and decaying plants in the soil. The chemical mix results in carbonic acid and forms acidic water. As this water flows through cracks in the ground, it seeps into the rock layer below the soil. Once the acidic water reaches carbonate rocks like limestone or marble, it dissolves the rock and creates openings, passageways, and cave formations.

With this experiment, you can create a model of a cave made through dissolution.

MATERIALS

- Clear glass or plastic bowl (big enough to hold at least 2 cups)
- Package of sugar cubes (representing the carbonate rocks)
- Modeling clay
- Fork
- Spray bottle filled with warm water

1. Line a glass bowl with sugar cubes. Press them up against the glass and pack them in tightly. You should be able to see the sugar cubes through the bowl. The bowl acts as the window to your cave.

2. Once you have placed the sugar cubes against the bottom and sides of the bowl, use clay to seal the cubes in place. Spread a layer of clay at least ⅛ inch (3 mm) thick over the sugar cubes and seal it around the sides of the bowl.

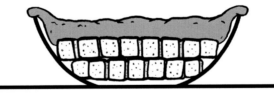

3. Use a fork to poke 15 to 20 holes in the clay all the way through the clay and sugar cubes. The holes represent the cracks in the soil and ground.

4. Water from a spray bottle represents acidic water. Spray the surface of the clay with warm water. Observe what happens to the sugar cubes. Over time, acidic water melts away limestone and marble to create caves, just like the warm water in the spray bottle is melting the sugar, leaving behind clay molds.

recognized Buckland as one of the top scientists in all of Europe.

Buckland's keen observation skills and deductive reasoning also helped him as he studied the remains of a monster-sized animal. Working with just the jaw, leg, shoulder, and hip bones, Buckland used his knowledge of anatomy to describe the animal he named *Megalosaurus*. It was a lizard-like creature, 30 feet long and 10 feet tall (9 meters long, 3 meters tall), and probably weighed about a ton (about as heavy as a compact car). Its dagger-shaped curved teeth were perfect for ripping the flesh of other animals. This **carnivore** was at the top of the food chain when it roamed the English landscape.

The *Megalosaurus* was introduced to the Geological Society of London in 1824 by Buckland. He unveiled this impressive lizard on the night he took over as the president of the society. It was the first genus of non-avian dinosaurs to be named.

Buckland's description of the massive meat-eating animal fascinated his fellow scientists and inspired deeper investigation into prehistoric life. Paleontology was quickly becoming a specialized science.

Buckland Family Fun

In 1825 when William Buckland was 41, he married naturalist and illustrator Mary Morland. Theirs was a match of equal intelligence and inquisitiveness.

Mary was born on November 20, 1797, in Abingdon-on-Thames, England. Her mother died while Mary was an infant, and her father quickly remarried. With a house full of half brothers and sisters, Mary was sent to live with Sir Christopher Page and his wife at Oxford. The Pages encouraged Mary's interest in science and art. As a teenager, she read the works of French scientist Georges Cuvier and became fascinated with fossils. A gifted illustrator and enthusiastic fossil collector, Mary provided Cuvier with specimens and detailed fossil illustrations.

William Buckland speaking in the Geological Lecture Room at Oxford. *Courtesy of the Metropolitan Museum of Art, Wikimedia Commons*

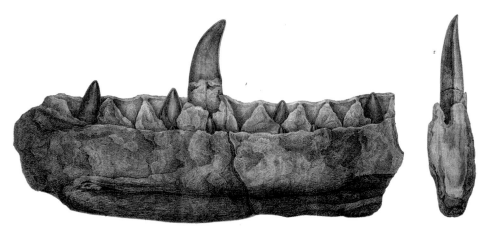

ANTERIOR EXTREMITY OF THE RIGHT LOWER JAW OF THE MEGALOSAURUS.
FROM STONESFIELD, NEAR OXFORD.

Scale of Inches

By the time Mary met William she was known as a well-educated naturalist and a fine illustrator. A story of their meeting was recorded in the diary of Miss Caroline Fox:

Dr. Buckland was once traveling somewhere in Dorsetshire, and reading a new and weighty book of Cuvier's which he had just received from the publisher; a lady was also in the coach, and amongst her books was this identical one, which Cuvier had sent her. They got into conversation, the drift of which was so peculiar that Dr. Buckland, at last, exclaimed "You must be Miss Morland, to whom I am about to deliver a letter of introduction." He was right, and she soon became Mrs. Buckland.

Mary and William took a yearlong geological trip for their honeymoon. They visited fellow geologist Georges Cuvier in Paris, toured museums, visited rock quarries and caves, and collected fossil and rock specimens. Returning home, they set up housekeeping in Christ Church at Oxford and had nine children. Five of them lived to adulthood.

The Buckland children were encouraged in nature and science studies. Each child had a personal collection of rocks, feathers, shells, leaves, and insects. The Bucklands also kept cages full of

Grow a Geode

Geologists like William Buckland and Georges Cuvier not only studied fossils but were also interested in minerals created in the **Earth's crust**. They understood that it took hundreds or even thousands of years for mineral crystals to grow in the earth. Mineral formation helped them understand that the fossils they were discovering had to have died and been buried thousands, perhaps millions, of years earlier.

You can study the process of crystal formation with this experiment. This is a recipe for two geodes. Increase it appropriately for the number you want to make.

ADULT SUPERVISION REQUIRED

MATERIALS

- 1 egg
- 2 small mixing bowls
- Paper towels
- Alum powder (in the spice section)
- White glue
- Paintbrush
- 2 cups (475 mL) hot water
- Glass measuring cup (large enough to hold at least 2 cups)
- 2 small glass jars, each large enough to hold half of an egg
- Food coloring

1. Carefully crack an egg in half and put the yolk and egg white in a small mixing bowl to be used for cooking. (You will not need the contents of the egg for this experiment.)

2. Wash the two halves of the eggshell and wipe them dry with a paper towel. Set the eggshells aside.

3. Place 2 tablespoons (30 mL) of alum powder into the other mixing bowl.

4. Now take white glue and drip some into each half of the eggshell. Spread the glue all over the inside surface of the shell with the paintbrush. Then liberally sprinkle alum powder on the inside of the eggshell so that all of the glue is covered by the powder.

5. Tap out any excess powder. Place the eggshells on a paper towel to dry overnight.

6. The next day, when the eggshells are completely dry, boil 2 cups (475 mL) of water and pour it into a glass measuring cup. Add ¾ cup (180 mL) of alum powder and stir until it is dissolved. Divide the mixture into the two glass jars and add 30 drops of food coloring to each jar. Let the mixture cool for about 20–30 minutes.

7. When the mixture is cool to the touch, carefully submerge one half-shell into each jar so that it sits at the bottom. Make sure the eggshell has the alum-coated side facing up. Let the shells sit in the solution for 15 hours.

8. Carefully remove the shells from the solution and set them on a paper towel to dry. If you want to grow bigger crystals leave them in the solution longer. You have just created a geode!

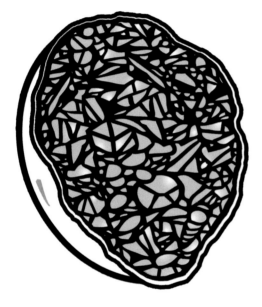

WHAT'S FOR SUPPER?

Dinner at the Buckland's home was a recipe for adventure. William believed that every animal was a potential food source and invented a diet he called *zoophagy*. It meant he would cook up any and every type of animal he could find. The Buckland children grew up eating everything from crocodile stew and roasted hedgehog to mice served on toast.

William believed it was his duty to explore different food sources and vowed to taste every animal on the Earth, or at least as many as he could get in his kitchen. Bear steaks were reportedly delicious, but the cooked mole was banished from the menu. It tasted terrible. William experimented and found that some insects made delightful snacks, but blue bottle flies were repulsive. Like moles, they were ejected from the serving list.

William became famous for his unusual diet, and stories were told about how he could identify the type of animal he was eating just by the taste. One story claims that when William was touring a cathedral in Italy, the guide showed him a dark spot on the floor that church members believed was the blood of a saint. William bent down and took a lick, then stood up and declared the stain was bat urine.

Legend has it that William ate his strangest snack when he was a guest of Lord Harcourt, the Archbishop of York. Lord Harcourt was passing around one of his prized possessions, a mummified piece of King Louis XIV's heart. When the relic was passed to William, he picked it up and popped it in his mouth. Apparently, he couldn't resist the opportunity to eat a king's heart.

Buckland family silhouette showing William and Mary, and their son Frank under the table.
Courtesy of Wikimedia Commons

William's son Frank followed in his father's footsteps both in becoming a famous scientist and in pursuing his hobby of eating through the animal kingdom. He was one of the founders of the British Acclimatisation Society, an organization that supported the introduction of new plants and animals as food sources. Frank hoped to transform odd or foreign meats into familiar household staples. The first dinner of the British Acclimatisation Society included a menu of sea slug and deer sinew soup, kangaroo stew, and Syrian pig. While the soups tasted a little glue-like, the pig and kangaroo were declared to be tasty, and the night was considered a success.

Unfortunately, Frank and his fellow scientists did not realize that introducing foreign plants and animals into new ecosystems would result in disaster. That's how Australia became infested with rabbits and why starlings are now an invasive species in the United States. Today there are laws that protect local ecosystems and laws that protect endangered species from becoming menu items.

snakes, frogs, and birds. Guinea pigs were known to run across the dining room table, and occasionally the pony took a stroll through the house.

Mary was always ready to lend a hand to William's experiments. Once when William was puzzled by some fossilized footprints, he asked Mary to roll out some dough on the table. He then brought in the pet tortoise and urged it to walk on the dough. This confirmed to William that the fossil footprints were certainly those of a prehistoric tortoise. Mary was probably the one who cleaned up the mess.

Fossil hunting was often a family expedition. All the children were well versed in fossil identification, extraction, and labeling. Trips to the Lyme Regis coast always included a visit with Mary Anning and some hunting expeditions.

In 1836, after years of research, William published his Bridgewater Treatise, *Geology and Mineralogy*. It was lavishly illustrated by Mary with detailed drawings of everything from fossil corals and crinoids to sharks and squid. Well received by the public, it brought to life ancient animals no human had ever seen.

William and Mary spent their lives exploring the fossil and rock formations of Europe. William even studied theories about **glaciers** with Louis Agassiz in Switzerland. William's ideas changed and evolved as science uncovered more facts. He became convinced that the rock surface deposits and formations were not caused by the Great Flood but were the result of glaciers forming and melting over the course of many years.

William died on August 14, 1856, at the age of 72. He suffered from a tubercular infection that spread to his brain and spent the last five years living in a sanatorium (long-term care hospital).

Mary died just a year later, on November 30, 1857. She was 60 years old. Mary kept researching to the very end and became fascinated with microscopes and investigating microbic marine life. The Bucklands' contributions to the advancement of paleontology were invaluable and are still considered by today's scientists.

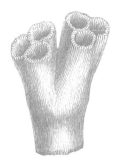

Examine Footprint Fossils

Trace fossils are the imprints or marks left by an organism, such as a footprint or a tunnel. Fossilized footprints or animal tracks are rare but valuable. Tracks can help paleontologists determine which animals lived in an area and how many might have traveled together. Fossil footprints can also tell the ages of different individuals (such as a mother with young). In addition, tail dragging marks help scientists understand an animal's body position when walking.

You can learn about footprint fossils with this fun but messy experiment. It is similar to the experiment William and Mary Buckland did with their children's pet tortoise.

Warning! You probably need to conduct this experiment outside to keep the adults in your home happy.

MATERIALS

* Adventurous friends
* Several pieces of butcher paper at least 4 feet (1.2 m) long or several pieces of white construction paper taped together in 4-foot lengths
* Nontoxic water-based paint (tempera, fingerpaints, or watercolors work well)
* 2-inch paintbrushes
* Bucket of water

1. Before you begin the experiment, talk about the different ways humans move. They can run, skip, walk, stomp, etc. Decide on several different movements you will use in making your trace footprint fossils.

2. Assign a movement to each person participating in the experiment. Some people can do more than one movement, but each movement should be done on a separate length of paper.

3. Lay the paper on the ground outside. You may need to anchor it if it is windy.

4. Use a brush to paint the soles of the bare feet of the first participant. Have that person walk, run, or jump—whatever their assigned motion may be—across the paper. After they have finished, have them clean their feet in the water bucket.

5. Repeat this with the next participant.

6. Once the papers are dry, bring them inside.

7. Lay out the tracks for everyone to examine. How are they different from each other? How does a running track compare to a walking track? Would the tracks

of prehistoric animals look different if they were running or walking? What can fossilized tracks tell paleontologists about the animals that lived millions of years ago?

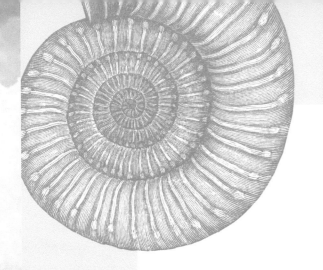

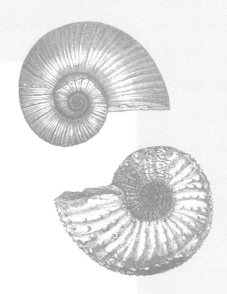

6

Georges Cuvier

In 1795, four years before Mary Anning was born, Georges Cuvier was appointed as the assistant chairman of animal anatomy at Jardin des Plantes, the natural history museum in Paris He was only 26 years old and was already well known for his keen scientific mind and his knowledge of animal taxonomy and classification.

Georges was born on August 23, 1769, in Montbéliard, France. The son of Lieutenant Jean George Cuvier and Anne Clemence Chatel, he

Portrait of Georges Cuvier. *Courtesy of Wikimedia Commons*

books and stories. Anne supplied all the books and articles she could get her hands on, which was difficult in the time before public lending libraries. She also instructed him in art. Georges was so talented in drawing that his mother had him tutored by a relative who was a professional architect. Learning and drawing would be his lifetime passions.

Classmates and teachers were all astounded at Georges's remarkable memory. He liked creating and memorizing lists of facts about everything from the kings of France to dates of battles and wars. It was said that once he read something, he never forgot it. For fun, Georges studied maps and redrew them on a miniature scale, then gave the tiny maps to his friends.

Curled up in a chair reading a book, any book, was Georges's favorite way to occupy the day. He spent so much time reading that his mother worried it would hurt his health and often shooed him out of the house, telling him to get some exercise. Georges spent his time outside observing nature. He was fascinated with birds, turtles, fish, foxes, rabbits, and any other creature he could spy.

When he was 10, Georges's mother enrolled him in the *gymnasium*, or local preparatory school. There he discovered the thrill of languages and quickly became proficient in both Latin and Greek. He also achieved honors in history, geography, and mathematics. As a young teenager, Georges formed a club for his classmates and appointed himself the president. They met every Thursday evening to discuss a topic of natural history or a book, or share their travels and learning

was christened Jean Leopold Nicolas Frederic Cuvier. He had an older brother named Georges who died as a toddler. Exactly like Mary Anning's parents, Georges's parents gave him the name of his dead brother. It was a common custom to remember the children who died by giving another child the same name.

Homeschooled by his mother, Georges loved learning, and by the age of four was devouring experiences. It was an early indication of the life Georges would lead as a professor and academic.

Cuvier was invited to attend the University of Stuttgart free of charge. This was an offer too good to refuse, so at the age of 14, he packed his bags and headed to Germany to begin his college career. He didn't know how to speak or read German, but that didn't stop Georges. By the end of his first term, he received the top academic prize for his mastery of the German language.

Finding the Truth About Fossils

During his studies at university, Cuvier became interested in geology. When he graduated at the age of 19, he took a position as a tutor for the son of a French nobleman in Normandy. In his spare time, Cuvier began a study comparing fossilized shells to shells and mollusks that were alive in the present day. His studies made him aware that there were gaps in the current way scientists classified animals. Cuvier hated gaps in logic and identified ways to improve the classification system. He wrote papers about his ideas and presented them to local scientific groups. His concepts attracted the attention of scientists in Paris, and in 1795 Cuvier packed his bags again and headed for Paris and the Jardin des Plantes.

Working with museum collections, Cuvier was able to investigate fossils from larger animals. Studying the fossilized bones of a mammoth elephant, Cuvier realized the fossil bones had distinct differences from modern elephants. He suggested the theory that perhaps these were a totally different species, one that was not alive on the Earth anymore.

Many fellow scientists scoffed at this idea. They were sure that these huge elephants must be hidden somewhere in the world, perhaps in the deepest, unexplored parts of the Amazon. Cuvier said this was ridiculous. The animals were just too large to not have been seen by humans. Besides, it was evident that the mammoth had adapted to living in a cold climate, not a tropical forest.

History proved Cuvier right. Living mammoths were never discovered, and modern scientists understand that 99 percent of all the species that ever existed on the Earth are now extinct. But these ideas were revolutionary during Georges Cuvier's and Mary Anning's lifetimes.

The next years were busy for Cuvier. He became known as the world's top **anatomist**. He dissected animal species from around the world, learning about the structure of birds, reptiles, and mammals. His keen eye and remarkable memory helped him see the similarities and differences in living animals compared to similar extinct species. He correctly speculated that at one time reptiles had been the dominant animal roaming the Earth.

Fossils discovered around Paris engrossed Cuvier. He studied the bones of animals that humans had never seen in Europe like rhinoceroses, giant hyenas, and hippopotamuses. Using the bones of living animals, he identified and named extinct species like *Megatherium*, a giant ground sloth that stood 20 feet (6 m) tall and weighed

Rock Cycle Experiment

Just like plants and animals have a life cycle from birth to death and decomposition, rocks also have a cycle. There are three main kinds of rocks: igneous, metamorphic, and sedimentary:

__Igneous rocks__ are formed from melted rock deep inside the Earth.
__Sedimentary rocks__ are formed from layers of sand, silt, dead plants, and animal skeletons.
__Metamorphic rocks__ are formed when other rocks are changed by heat and pressure underground.

You can demonstrate the rock cycle with this fun experiment.

ADULT SUPERVISION REQUIRED

MATERIALS

- Unwrapped Starburst candies (different colors)
- 3 sheets of aluminum foil, 8 inches × 8 inches (20 cm × 20 cm)
- 3 sheets of wax paper, 8 inches × 8 inches (20 cm × 20 cm)
- Toaster oven
- Oven mitt
- Plate
- Potato masher or meat hammer

1. Pick three different colors of Starburst and stack them on top of each other. The candies represent layers of different rocks.

2. Place an 8" × 8" sheet of aluminum foil on a table. Then put an 8" × 8" sheet of wax paper on top of the aluminum foil.

3. Place your stack of "rock layers" on the foil and wax paper. Fold the wax paper and foil over the stack of Starburst so the candy is covered.

4. Now use the heel of your hand to smash the candy flat. The pressure of your hand represents the pressure of the earth on the rocks. This is how a **sedimentary rock is created with time and pressure.**

5. Lay out another sheet of aluminum foil and put wax paper on top of it. Stack three different colored candies on top of each other and put them on the paper. Cover the candy stack with the foil and wax paper.

6. Have an adult place the candy stack in a toaster oven just long enough for the candy to become soft: 30 seconds or less at 325°F (160°C). The adult should then remove the candy stack with an oven mitt and set it on a plate.

7. With the help of an adult, use a meat hammer or potato masher to apply pressure to the candy stack. This represents how **heat and pressure work to form metamorphic rock.**

8. Once again, lay out the aluminum foil and place the wax paper on top. Stack three different colored candies on top of each other and place them in the center of the foil.

9. Have an adult place them in the toaster oven until they reach a liquid state and are completely melted: one minute at 350°F (175°C) or less. Have the adult remove the candies from the oven with the oven mitt and set them aside to cool. **Do NOT** touch them until they have cooled. Once the candy has hardened, it will **represent how igneous rock is formed.**

10. Once all the samples have cooled, look at the different formations. How is the sedimentary different from the metamorphic? How is it different for the igneous? Why do you think most fossils can be found in sedimentary rock?

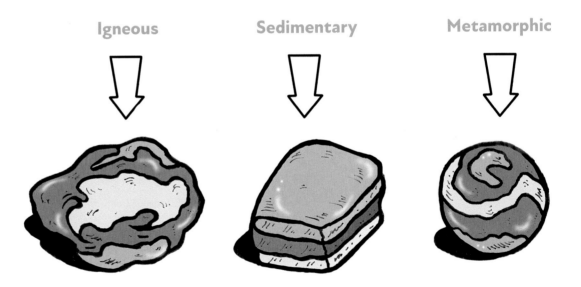

Igneous　　**Sedimentary**　　**Metamorphic**

The Fossil that Fooled Cuvier

In 1823 Cuvier was a well-respected scientist and author, having written numerous books on animal anatomy, fossils, mollusks, birds, and ancient Egypt. At 54 years of age, he was self-assured and confident in his superior scientific abilities. He was a councillor of the Napoleonic University of France and had been given the nobility title of baron in recognition of his achievements.

As an expert in anatomy, Cuvier understood that animals that walked on four legs had only seven vertebrae. Even the long-necked giraffe's spine contains just seven bones. Birds had more, varying between 13 and 25, and reptiles typically had between three and eight neck vertebrae.

In 1823 when Cuvier received a drawing of Anning's latest discovery, the plesiosaur, he immediately declared it a hoax. An animal with 35 neck vertebrae? Ridiculous. The amount of air needed to fill a trachea of a neck that long was impossible.

In his opinion, Anning was an uneducated young woman trying to earn money by perpetuating a fraud. She must have taken the head of a sea snake and added it to the body of an ichthyosaur. He pointed to a crack in the bone at the base of the neck as proof that this was a trick.

Anning was angry and frustrated. The opinion of the renowned Georges Cuvier could make or break her life. If Cuvier were proved right, her fossil business would be ruined. No one would trust her finds. And as a woman, she couldn't even argue her case in front of the Geological Society.

Megatherium—giant sloth—in the **British Natural History Museum.**
Photo by Darrell Bearce, courtesy of the British Natural History Museum

4 tons (3.6 metric tons), and *Palaeotherium*, which was an ancient relative of the modern okapi.

Cuvier became so good at anatomy and animal classification that he was able to correctly identify the first known flying reptile, the pterodactyl, from a drawing of its bones. Other scientists incorrectly thought it was a flying mammal related to a bat, but Cuvier recognized the bones were similar to a lizard.

She had to wait for her male friends to defend her work. If they failed, she would never work as a fossilist again.

Finally, in January 1824, a meeting of the Geological Society of London was convened. Scientists examined Anning's fossil and debated Cuvier's accusations. William Conybeare and Henry De la Beche testified about how they had been looking for the bones of just such an animal. The evidence of their and Anning's excavations and meticulous skeletal articulation convinced the scientists that the great Georges Cuvier had made a mistake.

A few months later, after Cuvier examined the bones of the plesiosaur himself, he admitted that he had rushed to judgment and was wrong. The bizarre creature was indeed what it seemed and was not a hoax. It was one of the few times Cuvier ever had to admit to making a mistake. And to Anning, that admission was the saving grace for her fossil business. If the great Georges Cuvier said Anning was right, she had the scientific stamp of approval.

Georges Cuvier died just eight years after his quarrel with Mary Anning. Before his death, Cuvier was named a Peer of France for life in honor of his scientific contributions. The title was only given to the greatest and highest-ranking members of the French nobility.

Today scholars recognize Cuvier as the founder of comparative anatomy and a cornerstone scientist in the building of vertebrate paleontology. He established the concept of *function over form* in the classification of animals. For example, because scientists understand that the function of claws is for ripping and tearing, if they find fossils of sharp claws, they'll know they belong to a carnivore. They'll also know that this animal will have had sharp, cutting teeth for attacking prey. Herbivores have flat teeth and no claws.

When scientists excavate piles of bones mixed together, the knowledge of anatomy helps them sort the bones. They match carnivore skulls with arms and legs that have claws. Herbivore skulls are matched with appendages that do not have claws.

Cuvier's ideas influenced generations of scientists and helped establish modern techniques used in fossil identification and naming. Cuvier was also a progressive thinker when it came to the education of women and saw no reason why they should not pursue careers in science. He encouraged his only daughter, Clementine Cuvier, to follow in his footsteps and work as his research assistant. Sadly, Clementine died in 1827 of tuberculosis. She was only 22 years old. Cuvier would be glad to know that many women have taken up the study of science and are making an impact through their ideas and discoveries.

Georges Cuvier died May 13, 1832, from cholera and was buried in the Cimetière du Père Lachaise in Paris. He was 62.

The Bone Wars

Paleontology can get dirty, and not just because fossils are buried in rocks and soil. During the late 1800s, two scientists turned fossil hunting into a down-and-dirty competition that involved insults, name-calling, bribery, and downright theft.

The scientists in question were Othniel Charles (O.C.) Marsh and Edward Drinker Cope, and their professional rivalry put American science on the world stage, but it ruined their personal lives.

Edward Cope was born into a wealthy Pennsylvania Quaker family in 1840. His father planned for Edward to become a gentleman farmer, but Edward declared farming a boring occupation and eventually convinced his father to allow him to attend college. He became fascinated with fossils and published his first scientific paper at age 19.

Before he could complete his university studies, the Civil War broke out. With America in turmoil and his education disrupted, Cope traveled to Europe, visiting museums and science institutions from Great Britain through Austria. While

in Berlin he met O.C. Marsh, who was studying at the University of Berlin. At first, the two men seemed to be the perfect companions. Marsh was nine years older and already held two university degrees, but Cope was a prolific author, having already published 37 scientific papers. They were both fascinated with fossils and prehistoric life. It should have been a friendship for the ages; instead, it devolved into a backstabbing catfight.

In 1866, when Marsh returned from his studies in Germany, he was appointed professor of vertebrate paleontology at Yale University. That same year, Marsh's wealthy uncle donated money to Yale to start the Peabody Museum of Natural History. Not surprisingly, Marsh was named one of the three original curators.

Cope returned home from Europe ready to discover American fossils. His studies had shown him what types of sedimentary rocks to look for, and he arranged to begin excavating in New Jersey's marl pits, local rock quarries that contained fossils from the Cretaceous Period, the third and final segment of the Mesozoic Era. Excited about the bones and teeth he was finding, Cope invited his friend Marsh for a visit.

The finds were indeed spectacular. Teeth and bones of a *Hadrosaurus* had been found at the site, and Marsh had a museum to fill. Behind Cope's back, Marsh made a deal with the local miners: he would pay them a premium if they would ship their best finds to him. When Cope figured out that the choicest fossils were being hijacked, he was beyond furious. But this was just the start of the war.

Othniel Charles (O.C.) Marsh and Edward Drinker Cope, the men who fought the Bone Wars. *Courtesy of Wikimedia Commons*

In 1868 Cope published a paper about the *Elasmosaurus*, a marine reptile. His drawing gave the animal a short neck and a long, tapering tail. Unfortunately, well-known naturalist Joseph Leidy pointed out that Cope placed the head on the wrong side. It should have had a long neck and a shorter tail.

Marsh never let Cope forget that mistake and called Cope's work inferior. He often pointed out that Cope lacked the university credentials for a PhD and insinuated that because of this none of Cope's work could be trusted. Perhaps some of Marsh's animosity was because of jealousy that Cope had his father's money to back his digs, while Marsh was dependent on financing from donors and sponsors.

Cope made it his life mission to show Marsh that he was a superior scientist and would do anything to prove it. The rivalry caused Cope to become suspicious of Marsh. He worried spies were infiltrating his digging expeditions, which proved true. But Cope also sent people to spy on Marsh's work. They raced to be the first to find the biggest and most bizarre animals.

Their competition yielded amazing discoveries: huge plant-eating dinosaurs nearly 80 feet (24 m) long, swimming birds with razor-sharp teeth, three-toed horses, and huge 13-foot-tall rhinos that wandered around grazing like cattle. The men were responsible for naming many famous dinosaurs including the *Triceratops*, *Stegosaurus*, *Apatosaurus*, and *Allosaurus*.

While their competition unearthed hundreds of new species of prehistoric animals, it also caused problems. Sometimes in their rush to outdo each other, they made mistakes. Big mistakes. The heads of some dinosaurs were matched with the wrong bodies. Dinosaurs that had already been named were declared a new species. Worst of all, their mistakes gave American paleontologists the reputation of being reckless and imprecise.

Sadly, Marsh and Cope's Bone Wars lasted throughout their lives. It ruined their finances, leaving both men to die alone in near poverty. In the end, Cope wanted to prove to Marsh that he was smarter. When he died in 1897, Cope asked that his brain be autopsied and measured. It was the belief at that time that larger brains equated to greater intelligence. Marsh didn't join in that last bit of competition and was buried near his beloved Peabody Museum. Cope's brain was preserved but never examined and remains in storage at the University of Pennsylvania.

The Crystal Park Dinosaurs

Today science centers and natural history museums around the world have life-size recreations of Mesozoic animals. Mechanical tyrannosaurs roar in dinosaur halls while stegosaurs munch on plants. Images of prehistoric animals are so familiar that preschool children can tell the difference between an *Iguanodon* and a *Spinosaurus*.

But in the 1850s, most people had no concept of how dinosaurs might have looked when they were alive. Museums exhibited some of the skeletons, and a few people may have seen some illustrations, but for most people it was hard to imagine

Make a Mesozoic Diorama

The ichthyosaur and plesiosaur fossils that Mary Anning discovered were animals that lived during the Mesozoic Era. This was a time when both the land and the ocean were full of large lizard-like creatures. Life looked very different from the world we see today.

To help people understand this world, museums often create scenes with three-dimensional plants and animals called dioramas. You can build a miniature diorama.

MATERIALS

- Books about Mesozoic time
- Pictures of Mesozoic plants and animals
- Shoebox or box of similar size
- Water-based paint
- Paintbrushes
- Construction paper
- Scissors
- Markers
- Tape
- Glue
- Modeling clay

1. Before you begin this project, spend time reading about the Mesozoic Era. Some of the animals from that time are described in this book. You can also check out books and videos from the library or investigate reliable websites, like those listed in the Resources section, pages 114–115.

2. Decide whether you want to create an ocean or land diorama, then select the plants and animals that you want to feature. Paint the inside of a shoebox or similarly sized box with colors that are appropriate for the topography. This will serve as the base for your diorama.

3. Get creative with construction paper, scissors, and markers to make plants and trees, or seaweed and kelp. Tape or glue them into the shoebox. Then use modeling clay to build your animals and add them to the diorama.

4. Complete your project by writing a description of the scene and labeling the plants and animals.

5. Show off your creation to friends and family to help them learn about the Mesozoic Era.

giant lizards roaming the Earth. That all changed in 1854 when a new park opened up on the south side of London.

Crystal Palace Park boasted the first life-size sculptures of dinosaurs in the world. Sculptor Benjamin Waterhouse Hawkins was hired to create these statues based on advice from dinosaur expert Richard Owen. The goal was to provide an educational experience for Londoners.

Waterhouse Hawkins designed the outdoor exhibit to have three islands, each representing a geological era with the appropriate animals. This would give viewers the impression of moving through time and observing the changes in animal species. Visitors could view a giant lizard dicynodont from the Paleozoic Era, ichthyosaurs and *Iguanodon* from the Mesozoic Era, and *Megatherium* (giant ground sloth) and *Megaloceros giganteus* (giant elk) from the Cenozoic Era.

Waterhouse Hawkins first built the creatures at full size out of clay. Then a mold was taken, allowing cement sections to be cast. The larger sculptures were hollow with a brickwork interior. The process took months of work and was quite expensive, but the public was amazed at the results.

Thousands of people flocked to the park astonished at the strange animals that had once roamed the Earth. It made *dinosaur* a household word and sparked interest in the prehistoric world.

Unfortunately, paleontology was a young science and new information was still being revealed. Within a few years of the park's opening, scientists discovered that many of the sculptures were

anatomically incorrect. The more fossil skeletons scientist found, the more they knew about the animals. For example, the *Megalosaurus* was sculpted to walk on all four legs, but scientists soon realized it walked upright using its hind legs. The statues of ichthyosaurs look like crocodiles when they were actually shaped more like dolphins.

But the inaccuracies didn't bother the public. Over a million people visited the exhibit each year. The exhibit expanded the minds of children and adults to imagine a world of animals that lived millions of years before. The success of the display encouraged museums to create full-size dioramas where people could view ancient life and cultures. It was the beginning of the "edutainment" industry that flourishes today with dinosaur theme parks and robotic replicas.

Today Benjamin Waterhouse Hawkins's sculptures are still on display in London. They have been cleaned and refurbished but have not changed in their inaccurate depiction of the animals. These first models serve as a tribute to how scientific knowledge changes and evolves with each discovery.

Benjamin Waterhouse Hawkins's *Iguanodon* sculptures in Crystal Palace Park. *Jes, courtesy of the artist, Wikimedia Commons, https://commons.wikimedia.org/wiki/File:Iguanodon_Crystal_Palace.jpg*

Rock Testing and Identification

Geologists like Cuvier used many different methods to identify the rocks and minerals they collected. Three of the basic methods are the Hardness Test, the Streak Test, and the Cleavage Test. You can experiment with each of these tests to learn the identity of rocks and minerals.

HARDNESS TEST

The Mohs Hardness Scale was invented in 1812 by German mineralogist Friedrich Mohs. This scale ranks minerals according to how easily they can scratch or be scratched by other materials.

MATERIALS

* Samples of minerals
* Fingernails
* Penny
* Nail
* Piece of ceramic tile (from hardware store)
* Journal

1. Test each of your specimens by scratching it first with your fingernail. If that doesn't make a mark on your mineral, try a penny, then a nail. And finally, use the mineral to try to scratch a piece of ceramic tile. The hardest minerals can scratch or cut the tile. Consult a rock and mineral identification guide to understand which minerals exhibit each hardness.

2. Record what you've discovered about each rock in your journal.

MOHS HARDNESS SCALE

Example mineral	Mohs Hardness Scale	Observations about the mineral
Talc	1	Easily scratched by fingernail
Gypsum	2	Can be scratched by fingernail
Calcite	3	Can be scratched with penny
Fluorite	4	Easily scratched with nail
Apatite	5	Scratched with nail with difficulty
Orthoclase	6	Can scratch ceramic tile with difficulty
Quartz	7	Scratches tile easily
Topaz	8	Scratches tile very easily
Corundum	9	Cuts tile
Diamond	10	Used as a tile or glass cutter

STREAK TEST

A streak test is another tool scientists use to determine the identity of a mineral. The streak is the color of the mineral in powdered form. Some minerals have the same streak color as their exterior, while others have a very different color.

MATERIALS

- ⭐ Samples of rocks or minerals
- ⭐ White streak plate—a piece of white ceramic tile (from hardware store)
- ⭐ Black streak plate—a piece of black ceramic tile
- ⭐ Journal

1. Choose one of your samples to test. Typically, it works best to test dark-colored specimens on the light tile and light-colored specimens on the dark tile.

2. Gently scratch the stone against the tile. The harder the sample, the harder you will need to press.

3. Observe the color of the streak and write it in your journal. Then use a rock and mineral identification guide to understand which minerals have what color streak.

Example mineral	Streak Color
Barite	White
Bauxite	White, but can be pink, brown, or red from iron stain
Calcite	White
Copper	Red
Diamond	Colorless
Galena	Lead gray to black
Gold	Metallic yellow
Malachite	Green
Marcasite	Grayish to black
Pyrite	Greenish black to brown
Quartz	Colorless
Silver	Slivery white
Sulfur	Yellow
Talc	White to pale green
Zircon	Colorless

CLEAVAGE TEST

In geology, *fracture* and *cleavage* are used to describe how minerals break apart when they are hit with a hammer. Minerals that have cleavage break into flat surfaces that reflect light. If pressure is put on a crystal and it breaks but retains a shape that is smooth and geometrical looking, this means it has cleavage.

Minerals that crumble or break into rough irregular shapes do not have cleavage and are said to have fracture. Fracture and cleavage help rock collectors identify the type of mineral they have found.

It is simple to test for cleavage.

ADULT SUPERVISION REQUIRED

MATERIALS

* Safety goggles
* Rock and mineral samples
* Small hammer
* Journal

1. This rock test should be done outside with an adult, and everyone nearby should wear safety goggles to protect their eyes from flying mineral particles. Place the rock sample on a hard surface and gently tap it with the hammer until it cracks.

2. Examine the sample. Did it crumble? Did it break into pieces with smooth sides?

3. If it crumbled, your sample is probably a rock rather than a mineral. Minerals tend to have cleavage; they break into pieces with some smooth edges. Use a mineral identification guide to learn more about cleavage and record any conclusions in your journal.

EXAMPLES OF MINERALS WITH CLEAVAGE

Mica: Exhibits excellent one-directional cleavage and pulls apart like sheets of paper

Feldspars: Have good two-directional cleavage and break apart at smooth 90-degree angles like the corner of a box

Galena: Has three-directional cleavage and breaks apart into cubes

Calcite: Has three-directional cleavage that forms 105-degree and 75-degree angles and breaks apart in the shape of a rhombus

Fluorite: Has four-directional cleavage called *octahedral cleavage* and forms a diamond-like shape

7

Female Fossilists:
Bone Finders and Barrier Breakers

Mary Anning had a significant impact on the young science of paleontology. Her fossil discoveries forced scholars to confront the theory of extinction and forever changed the concept of prehistoric times. But Anning wasn't the only woman fascinated with fossils. Anning's friends Elizabeth Philpot, Charlotte Murchison, and Mary Buckland all collected and researched fossils. None of them received recognition

Lyme Regis, home of Elizabeth Philpot and her sisters. *Photo by Darrell Bearce, courtesy of the photographer*

for their work, because in the 1800s science careers and higher education were not open to women.

This didn't stop Anning or her friends. They became self-educated scientists, reading articles, conducting their experiments, and corresponding with like-minded men and women. Their collections eventually ended up in some of the greatest museums and educational facilities in the world and are still studied by paleontology students today. The pioneering women of paleontology opened doors and minds with their tireless work.

Elizabeth Philpot

Elizabeth Philpot was born on July 5, 1779, 20 years before Mary Anning. Elizabeth was born into an upper-class English family and at the age of 29 moved with her sisters Mary and Margaret to Lyme Regis. Their brother John, a London solicitor (lawyer), purchased a house and provided a living for them as was the custom for families of well-to-do single women. None of the sisters ever married, and they spent the rest of their lives in Morely Cottage at the top of Broad Street.

The Philpot sisters became active in Lyme Regis, attending church, helping with charities, and mixing up batches of their homemade medicine. It was a soothing salve made with local herbs and was used for cuts, scrapes, burns, rashes, or any other skin complaint. Many of the people in Lyme Regis were too poor to pay for a doctor and were grateful to have something to help with their aches and pains.

Portrait of Elizabeth Philpot. *Courtesy of Wikimedia Commons*

The sisters kept busy, but young women with intelligent, curious minds couldn't help but become interested in the fossil bones, shells, and plants they found on their walks along the beaches and hills. They also noticed the young girl who scrambled up and down the beach each day, filling her bag with bits of rock and shell. Being neighborly, they struck up a conversation.

Elizabeth Philpot must have been impressed by Mary Anning's knowledge of the ammonites, belemnites, and vertebrae they found on their walks. The two became good friends despite their age and socioeconomic differences. Philpot was old enough to be Anning's mother, and perhaps she filled in some gaps of care and attention when Anning's mother was too busy or depressed to give her daughter much time.

Anning's discovery of the *Ichthyosaurus* brought international attention to the sleepy town of Lyme Regis. Now there were visitors combing the beaches and excavating in the hills long after the tourist season was over. Anning and Philpot became acquainted with scientists William Buckland, William Conybeare, and Henry De la Beche. They both wrote letters to the scientists telling of their discoveries and exchanging ideas about the fossils they uncovered, but Anning and Philpot had distinctly different motives for their collecting. Philpot had the luxury of finding specimens that she kept for her family's private collection, while Anning needed to excavate fossils to keep her family fed and housed. It was Anning's passion and her business. For Philpot, it was a passion and a hobby.

Through reading articles and books and talking with scientists, Philpot gained extensive knowledge about the animals that swam in the sea that once covered Lyme Regis. She enjoyed sharing her knowledge with all who were interested, including the adults and children in Lyme Regis. Upon request, Philpot and her sisters would allow visitors to examine their collection. Philpot carefully labeled each specimen with its scientific identification and wrote a detailed description of what the extinct animal looked like when it was alive.

Their collection was well known for the large collection of fossilized fish. The Philpots also found a plesiosaur skull, many different types of fossilized teeth, crinoids, and a small ichthyosaur skeleton. The sisters all contributed to the collection, but it was Elizabeth Philpot who communicated with scientists and the public.

The collection was so extensive that acclaimed English naturalist James Sowerby visited the Philpot home to examine the specimens, as did Richard Owen, the scientist famous for inventing the word *dinosaur*, and Swiss scientist Louis Agassiz.

Louis Agassiz was so grateful for the help he received from Mary Anning and Elizabeth Philpot that he named a fossil fish species after Philpot, *Eugnathus philpotae*, and two fish after Anning: *Acrodus anningiae* and *Belenostomus anningiae*.

When Mary Anning and William Buckland were asking the question whether belemnite fossils might have had ink sacs, like modern squid, it was Philpot who figured out how to rehydrate the fossilized ink sacs. Philpot used the ink to make sepia drawings of ichthyosaur and belemnite fossils. She started a craze that was followed by many artists in the area. Tourists could buy a picture of a prehistoric animal drawn with ink from a prehistoric fossil. It was a popular souvenir.

Although Philpot was older than her friend, Mary Anning, she outlived her by 10 years. She also lived longer than both of her sisters. It must have been hard for Elizabeth Philpot to say goodbye to her closest life companions.

After Philpot died in 1857, the entire Philpot collection was donated to the Oxford University Museum of Natural History. During their lifetime, the Philpot sisters amassed an amazing

Explore Erosion

The cliffs near Anning and Philpot's home were made of soft rocks and soil that were constantly eroding. The waves from the ocean and the storms caused the rock to break and crumble. It constantly exposed new layers of rock and fossils, but it also washed valuable soil into the sea. You can experiment to see the effects of erosion and how it impacted fossil hunting for Anning and Philpot.

MATERIALS

* 2 rimmed cookie sheets; 9" × 13" (23 cm × 33 cm) works well
* Enough soil to fill one of the cookie sheets
* A small section of sod or grass, the same size as a cookie sheet (from a garden or home improvement store)
* 2 blocks of scrap wood, each about 3 inches (8 cm) long
* Watering can or 1-gallon (3.8 L) plastic jug with holes punched in the bottom

1. This experiment is messy. It's a good idea to take the project outside. First, cover one cookie sheet with ½ inch (1.3 cm) of soil. Smooth the dirt so it is even and pat it down.

2. Place sod on the other cookie sheet. Pat down the sod so it is firmly in place.

3. Prop up one end of each pan on the blocks of wood.

4. Fill up a watering can or jug. Pour the water over the soil that does not have grass. Watch what happens.

5. Now pour the water on the pan with the sod. What happens? This shows that grass and plants protect soil and rocks from moving or eroding. In areas where the unprotected rocks and soil are exposed to water, they wash away. This is erosion.

400 fossils. In addition to this impressive collection of specimens, the museum also houses Philpot's correspondence. Today scholars from around the world visit the museum to view the specimens and read Philpot's letters to gain insight into the life of a paleontologist pioneer.

Charlotte Murchison

Charlotte Hugonin Murchison was born in 1788 to a wealthy, scientifically minded family. Her father, General Francis Hugonin, studied astronomy, while her mother, Charlotte Edgar Hugonin, excelled in botany. It was no wonder that Charlotte became fascinated with nature and, in particular, geology. Unfortunately, Charlotte's husband, Roderick Murchison, was more interested in horses and fox hunting. This was not how Charlotte planned to spend her life or her money.

Married in 1815, Charlotte set out on a campaign to reeducate her husband and convince him that he should use his time and money for the pursuit of science. Their honeymoon included a tour of France, the Alps, and Italy, where Charlotte used her remarkable artistic skills to record the plants and rock formations they saw on their journey. While they were in Italy, Charlotte contracted malaria and nearly died. It plagued her health for the rest of her life, but it didn't stop her studies of geology.

Charlotte studied on her own for nearly nine years. She attended lectures given by famous scientists Charles Lyell and Sir Humphry Davy. She studied chemistry, geology, and biology, and

became friends with the famous Scottish scientist Mary Somerville, who remarked that Charlotte was a rare woman for her time because she studied and understood science.

Finally, after nine years of dragging Roderick on rock-collecting expeditions, introducing him to scientists, and promoting the idea of a science career, Charlotte finally convinced him. They became a geology team, with Charlotte supporting and tutoring her husband throughout his career.

In the fall of 1825, Charlotte and Roderick took a trip to the southwest of England to explore the geology of the coast and see the fossils they had read about. When they arrived at Lyme Regis, Charlotte was suffering from exhaustion due to her malaria, and needed rest. Roderick, who was now keen on geology, left Charlotte to recover at the hotel, where she spent time with the local "fossilist" Mary Anning.

Anning and Murchison had a grand time. For once Anning met a woman who could speak her language. They discussed rock layers, fossil shells, teeth, and vertebrae. Murchison appreciated Anning's sharp mind and practical knowledge. And as Murchison beagn to feel stronger, the two went fossil hunting. Anning gave Murchison tips on how to locate the layers of sedimentary rock where fossils were most likely to be found. This trip made them friends for life. They frequently wrote letters to each other, and the one trip Anning took away from Lyme Regis to London was at Murchison's invitation.

With Charlotte's help and encouragement, Roderick began to present papers to the Geological

Illustration of *Ischadites koenigii*, similar to the fossil illustrations Charlotte Murchison created.
Courtesy of Wikimedia Commons

Society. Scholars argue that using today's publishing guidelines, Charlotte would certainly have been listed as a coauthor on most of Roderick's work. Charlotte accompanied Roderick on many of his geological expeditions, helping collect and identify specimens and illustrating many of their finds.

Not only did Charlotte help Roderick's academic work, but she also threw great parties. When her mother died, Charlotte received a large inheritance that was hers alone. She chose to use some of her funds to host huge gatherings, sometimes for as many as 700 people. She invited people who wouldn't normally cross paths, mixing politicians and high society with researching scientists and museum directors. She aimed to promote the popularity of science in society. Her parties also helped scientists and academics raise funds for their research projects.

Charlotte firmly believed in a woman's right to education. One of her good friends was geologist Charles Lyell. They had studied rock formations across Europe together, so Charlotte was surprised when Charles refused to let her, or any woman, attend his lectures at King's College London. The next time Charles lectured, Charlotte showed up with 300 of her friends, both male and female, to protest the rule. Charles gave in and allowed women to attend.

Charlotte's influence on early paleontology will never be fully known. Like many wives of the time period who assisted or even spearheaded their husbands' research, her contributions remain hidden.

Charlotte died in 1860 at her home in Belgravia, London, the site of her many wonderful parties. She was 80 years old.

Annie Alexander

Annie Montague Alexander was born in 1867, just a few years after Charlotte Murchison's death, but the world Alexander grew up in was vastly different from the time of Charlotte Murchison and Mary Anning. Women were making strides in gaining rights, including the right to attend university and study paleontology.

Annie was the granddaughter of missionaries who settled in Hawaii in 1832. Her father was Samuel Thomas Alexander, who was a successful sugar plantation owner. Annie's childhood was spent outdoors, tending the family garden, helping with the chickens, and playing in the bright Hawaiian sunshine. A daring child, Annie loved digging in caves, exploring the rain forest, and collecting anything from insects to rocks. Annie made everything into an adventure, including how she entered her bedroom. Instead of using a door, she preferred to climb onto the roof and go in through the window.

Annie also had a knack for business and was willing to work hard. Her uncle Henry wanted some avocado seedlings and told Annie he'd pay her 25 cents for each seedling she could obtain. Annie took the challenge and brought her uncle an oxcart filled with avocado seedlings, each one planted in a tin can. She also gave him a bill for $75. (That's about $2,000 in today's money.)

When Annie was 15, her family left Hawaii and moved to California. She went to boarding school in Massachusetts and toured Europe with her family. One of her most memorable adventures was going on a 1,600-mile (2,600 km) bicycle tour of England, France, and Spain with her father and sister. She traveled with her father to New Zealand, Hong Kong, China, and Japan. She also spent time exploring and camping in Oregon and California, where she studied birds and plants and became an excellent photographer.

In 1901 Annie began attending paleontology lectures given by John Merriam at the University of California, Berkeley. Fascinated with the stories of extinct mammals and reptiles found in Northern California, Annie wanted to go on a collecting expedition. She asked Merriam if she could come along and offered to pay for the entire expedition.

John Merriam probably thought she was kidding, or crazy. What young woman would have that kind of money? And how many young women wanted to spend the summer camping in the heat and dust with no modern conveniences?

Annie managed to convince the professor she was serious and that her bank account was amply supplied. That summer she took part in Merriam's fossil hunting expedition in Oregon. The next two summers she paid for expeditions to Shasta County, California, and the West Humboldt Range in Nevada.

Annie Alexander was fully involved in the digs. She learned how to mark and wrap bones, and how to clean fossils. She also gathered firewood, started the fires, and cooked the meals for the

Annie Alexander.
Courtesy of Wikimedia Commons

team. Alexander's spirit of adventure followed her into the field. She was always willing to crawl into the cracks and crevices no one had explored. Her explorations paid off, and during her second summer, she discovered three fossil lizards. The next summer she uncovered a never-before-seen reptile from the Triassic Period, the earliest segment of the Mesozoic Era. Professor Merriam named the reptile after Alexander, calling it *Thalattosaurus alexandre*.

Quicksand and Tar Pits

Some of the best-preserved prehistoric animals in the world have been found in California's La Brea Tar Pits. The early excavation of the pits happened between 1905 and 1915, when Annie Alexander was working to open the Museum of Vertebrate Zoology in Berkeley, California. She must have been fascinated by the discoveries that were made.

Fifty thousand years ago, during the Ice Age, animals accidentally wandered into the sticky tar, became stuck, and sank to their death. Their bones were preserved in the sticky substance. The same thing happened to dinosaurs that died in quicksand in Utah. These skeletons have been well preserved and provide paleontologists with incredible information about the animals, their hunting habits, and the prey they were chasing when they died.

You can make models of quicksand and tar pits with the following recipes. But a warning: this experiment is messy!

PART I:
QUICKSAND RECIPE

MATERIALS

* 2 cups (480 mL) cornstarch
* Mixing bowl
* Food coloring (this is just for fun)
* 1 cup (240 mL) warm water
* Fork or spoon for stirring
* Paper plate
* Plastic dinosaurs

1. Place 2 cups of cornstarch in the mixing bowl.

2. Add a couple of drops of food coloring to 1 cup of warm water and stir.

3. Pour the water into the cornstarch slowly, stirring the whole time.

4. Once you have the contents completely mixed, start experimenting. Touch the "quicksand" mixture. How does it feel?

5. Plunge your hands into the quicksand and play with it. Does it feel like a liquid? Or does it feel like a solid? Poke it quickly and then poke it slowly. Does it react differently?

6. Pour a small amount of the quicksand onto the paper plate. Touch it. How does it feel? When combined, cornstarch and water do not make a normal liquid. They form a *suspension*. This means that the grains of starch have not dissolved like grains of salt or sugar do when combined with water. The grains of cornstarch are just suspended and spread out in the water. If you let the mixture sit for a while, the cornstarch will separate from the water and settle at the bottom of the bowl. The size and shape of the cornstarch grains cause the cornstarch to lock up and hold its shape when pressure is applied. This is

exactly how quicksand works. It appears to be a solid layer of sand, but it's not.

7. Now place toy dinosaurs gently on top of the "quicksand" and watch what happens. Animals that encounter quicksand sink as they struggle. The quicksand helps preserve their bones.

PART 2:
TAR PIT RECIPE

Tar pits act differently. The animals walk into the tar and get stuck. They die, and then their bodies sink into the tar. You can simulate the tar pits with this recipe. Once again, be aware that this gets messy!

MATERIALS

* 1 cup (240 mL) white school glue
* Mixing bowl
* Food coloring
* Spoon
* 1 cup (240 mL) liquid starch
* Plastic dinosaurs

Illustration of prehistoric animals sinking in the La Brea Tar Pits.
Robert Bruce Horsfall, courtesy of Wikimedia Commons

1. Put 1 cup of glue in a mixing bowl and add several drops of food coloring. Use a spoon to mix it completely.

2. Pour 1 cup of starch into the mixing bowl and use your hands to combine the liquids. The glue and starch will form a thick, slimy substance like the tar pits.

3. Let the "tar" settle in your bowl. It will have a smooth, flat surface.

4. Set a few toy dinosaurs on top of the "tar" and watch what happens. Just as the toys sink into the tar, so did the prehistoric animals.

In 1906 Alexander met naturalist Joseph Grinnell, who ran a small research museum out of the parlor of his home. Grinnell and Alexander agreed that the West Coast needed a natural history museum to study the rapidly vanishing plants and animals of the region. Alexander decided that if a museum was needed, she would build it. With her financial support, the Museum of Vertebrate Zoology was opened in 1908 at the University of California, Berkeley, with Joseph Grinnell as the director.

Paleontology was not Alexander's only passion; she also loved finance and admitted that she spent much of her spare time poring over the financial pages instead of reading the novels or magazines that were considered appropriate for women at the time.

Alexander understood the real value of an investment. When a friend tried to talk her into buying into a lucrative business that promised large returns, she refused. Instead, she took him to the museum and showed him the groups of students, declaring they were her investments.

Money wasn't Alexander's only contribution to the museum. Over the years she collected and donated over 20,000 specimens to the university's museums. Several species of living and fossil organisms were named after her, including *Hydrotherosaurus alexandrae*, a Cretaceous plesiosaur; *Swollenia alexandrae*, a rare grass species; *Shastasaurus alexandrae*, a Triassic ichthyosaur; and several others.

She worked in the field all her life and celebrated her 80th birthday working on an expedition to the Sierra de la Laguna in Baja, California. She died in 1950 at the age of 83. Not only did she establish the Museum of Zoology, but she also founded the University of California Museum of Paleontology and helped expand public higher education so all could have the opportunity to learn.

Dame Maria Ogilvie Gordon

Maria Gordon achieved what Mary Anning longed for: recognition by her peers and the opportunity to study. Born into a bustling family of eight children, Maria had the advantage of having a father who was the headmaster of Robert Gordon's College in Aberdeen, Scotland. Unlike Mary Anning, she grew up in a home that was financially secure, with parents who were well educated. They could make sure Maria and her sibling received the best education possible.

When she was nine, Maria was sent to boarding school at the Merchant Company Edinburgh Ladies' College. She enjoyed all of her studies, but science and music were her favorites. Bright and enthusiastic, Maria was named both head girl and best academic pupil.

At 18 she had to decide whether to study music or science. A gifted pianist, she chose music, but after only a year of study, she changed her mind. Science was the career she wanted. In 1890, she graduated from University College London with a bachelor's degree specializing in botany and zoology.

In the summer of 1891, she traveled with geologist Baron Ferdinand von Richthofen to the Dolomite Mountains to study geology. After five weeks of hiking through the mountains and examining fossil corals and shells, Maria was hooked. She decided to get her advanced degree in geological and paleontological research. The University of Berlin was her first choice, but they refused to accept her. Women were not allowed to study for higher-level degrees.

Frustrated, Maria moved on to the University of Munich, where she was permitted to continue her research but was not allowed to enter lecture halls. To hear the lectures, she had to find an empty room that was close and sit in there with the door half open, eavesdropping on the professor's talk. It was a hard way to get an education, but eventually she succeeded.

Four years of climbing the treacherous hills of the Dolomites collecting fossilized corals and mollusks paid off for Maria. Her paper published on the geology in southern Tyrol was so exceptional that in 1893 she was awarded a doctor of science in geology degree from the University of London, the very first woman to receive this degree.

In 1895 Maria accepted a proposal of marriage from her longtime admirer Dr. John Gordon, a physician from Aberdeen. John was proud of his wife's academic interests and encouraged her to continue her research. They raised three children and often did fieldwork as a family.

Maria published more than 30 scientific papers in her lifetime and in 1932 was awarded the Lyell Medal for exceptional contribution to the scientific community. Maria died in 1939 at the age of 75.

Maria Ogilvie Gordon. *George Grantham Bain Collection, Library of Congress, courtesy of Wikimedia Commons*

GEOLOGIC TIME

One billion is a huge number. If you wanted to count to a billion and you started counting this very minute and never went to sleep the whole time you were counting, it would take you over 30 years to reach 1 billion.

The history of the Earth is measured in billions of years and is called *geologic time*. Around 4 billion years ago, the Earth's crust hardened over the inner hot thick *mantle*. The cooling crust became solid, forming the very first rocks. As time passed, more layers of rock formed. Animals lived, died, and were buried in layers of rock. These layers of rocks and fossils are what scientists use to organize the geologic time scale.

Geologic time is organized into sections based on important changes found in the rock layers. The largest time intervals are called *eons*, with each eon being made up of millions of years. Within each eon, there are *eras* that begin and end with the rise of certain types of plants and animals and end when they decrease in number or become extinct.

Hadean Eon: This is the earliest eon, which began with the formation of the Earth. It began 4.6 billion years ago. This eon has no fossils. During this time, the surface temperature of the Earth was hot enough to melt rock, and there was no life.

Archean Eon: As the Earth's crust cooled, continents formed, and the first signs of life appeared. This eon lasted from 4 billion to 2.5 billion years ago.

Proterozoic Eon: During this eon, photosynthetic bacteria appeared, and early single-cell life-forms developed. It began 2.5 billion years ago.

Phanerozoic Eon: Visible life developed during this eon, including trees, dinosaurs, turtles, sloths, and humans. It began 541 million years ago and has lasted to the present. The Phanerozoic Eon is divided into three eras: Paleozoic, Mesozoic, and Cenozoic:

Paleozoic Era: In this era, complex **invertebrate** animals appeared. These animals had protective shells and exoskeletons. Examples are the trilobites, a group of arthropods similar to horseshoe crabs that ranged in size from as small as a dime to the size of a car tire. Crinoids, also known as sea lilies, were animals that looked like plants. They attached themselves to the seafloor like a coral and ate by filtering sea plankton out of the water with their feather-like arms. This era began 542 million years ago and lasted until 250 million years ago.

Mesozoic Era: A humid tropical climate with lush green plants brought in the Mesozoic Era. Dinosaurs started out as small animals but grew to gigantic proportions. This was the era of the *T. rex*, *Stegosaurus*, *Ichthyosaurus*, and *Plesiosaurus*. Pterodactyls ruled the air, and fast-running small mammals developed. It lasted from 250 to 65 million years ago.

Cenozoic Era: The climate changed quickly from a tropical one to an Ice Age. Dinosaurs and their reptilian relatives died out, allowing the small mammals to adapt and expand their territory. Giant fern trees died and were replaced with temperate forests of *deciduous trees* that shed their leaves seasonally. Mammoths and saber-toothed tigers roamed the Earth until they died out and were replaced with today's elephants, tigers, lions, and humans. The era lasted from 65 million years ago to the present.

Tilly Edinger

How can you possibly examine the brain of a dinosaur? Only hard substances like bones, claws, and teeth fossilize. All the soft tissues, like eyes, hearts, and brains, have long disintegrated.

For decades paleontologists believed the only way they could learn about the brains of extinct animals was by comparing them to similar living animals. But Tilly Edinger changed the world of paleontology forever when she discovered that animal brains left imprints on the fossilized skulls. She became the founder of the science of paleoneurology.

Born November 13, 1897, in Frankfurt, Germany, Johanna Gabrielle Ottilie (Tilly) Edinger was the youngest daughter of a wealthy Jewish family. Her father, Ludwig Edinger, was a neurologist who founded Frankfurt's first neurological research institute. Her mother, Anna Goldschmid Edinger, was a prominent social activist and feminist.

Tilly was tutored by governesses until she was 12, and then entered the Schiller-Schule secondary school. In 1909 it was the only secondary school for girls in the whole town. During her teen years, Tilly began to lose her hearing. Her parents had her fitted with hearing aids, but her hearing continued to decline throughout her life. She made it a point to sit at the front of the classroom so she could watch the instructors as they lectured.

A natural student, Edinger was fascinated with prehistoric life. It was while she was working on her doctoral dissertation that she came across the

Nothosaurus marchicus KOKEN, 1893

head of a marine reptile that had a preserved cast of the brain inside the skull. Edinger began studying skulls in collections across Europe and North America and discovered numerous brain impressions preserved inside skulls. The fossil casts of these brains allowed scientists to gain a deeper understanding of prehistoric animals and their brain development.

Unfortunately for Tilly, her family did not recognize her brilliance. Her father didn't believe women should pursue professional careers, and her mother thought that the study of fossils was just a hobby. And because her father wouldn't permit her to work as a paid paleontologist, Tilly decided she would become a volunteer. Her family's wealth meant she did not have to earn a paycheck. Tilly worked as a volunteer researcher at the Geological Institute of Frankfurt.

Nothosaurus was one of the dinosaurs Tilly Edinger studied that led to her discovery of brain casts. *Photo by Ghedoghedo, courtesy of the photographer, Wikimedia Commons, https://commons.wikimedia.org/wiki/File: Nothosaurus_marchicus_784.jpg*

After the Nazis came to power in Germany in 1933, it became increasingly difficult for Jewish scientists like Edinger. The Nazis wanted all Jewish people fired from professional jobs. Being a volunteer worked to Tilly's advantage; her boss kept her work a secret from the Nazis. They removed her nameplate from her office, and Edinger quietly entered the building through a side door. It worked for five years. But after the horrible Nazi raids and killing of Jewish people on the night of Kristallnacht, Edinger was discovered and had to leave.

With the help of friends, she escaped Germany and sailed for England, where she stayed while she was waiting for a visa that would allow her to continue on to the United States. Arriving in New York in 1940, Tilly took her first official paid position working as a researcher for the Harvard Museum of Comparative Zoology. In December of that year, Edinger was at the founding meeting of the Society of Vertebrate Paleontology. She was the only woman. She was elected as the first female president of the society in 1963.

Throughout her life, Tilly Edinger was recognized as a pioneering scientist. She was honored with a Guggenheim Foundation Fellowship and elected a fellow of the American Academy of Arts and Sciences, and she published three important books on prehistoric brains and skulls.

Tilly could have given up when she faced hearing loss, or when her father discouraged her career, or when the Nazis took over her country. But Tilly fought for her right to study, learn, and be free. At the end of her life, Edinger was completely deaf. When she was 69, she was struck by a truck that she did not hear coming toward her. She died from her injuries in 1967.

Her legacy as a diligent and inspired paleontologist lives on today. Scientists still rely on her fundamental research and the discovery of brain casts in skulls. Her final book, *Paleoneurology 1804–1966*, was completed by her colleagues after her death, and is considered the essential starting point for any project in paleoneurology.

Build a Plaster Jacket

Paleontologists use plaster jackets to safely transport fossils from the field to the lab. Fossils are quite fragile, and bumping around in the bed of a truck or the back of a trailer can easily destroy precious artifacts. Wrapping or sealing the fossils in a coating of plaster will stabilize them during travel. Once the fossil reaches the laboratory, the paleontologist removes the plaster jacket and can begin work on cleaning and articulating the specimen.

In this activity, you can practice making a plaster jacket. The protective jacket is made by dipping strips of burlap in plaster of Paris and wrapping the strips around the fossil.

MATERIALS

- Trash bags
- Scissors
- Piece of burlap cloth
- Objects to use as fossils: seashells, buttons, pencils, craft sticks, small stones, or any small toy
- Aluminum foil
- Nitrile gloves (plaster of Paris can dry out your skin)
- Safety goggles
- Plaster of Paris mix
- Water

1. Use trash bags to cover your work surface. This will make cleaning up much easier.

2. Use scissors to cut scraps of burlap into 1-inch (25 mm) strips.

3. Wrap your "fossil" in a protective layer of aluminum foil.

4. Wearing nitrile gloves and safety goggles, mix plaster of Paris with water according to the directions on the package. When it is ready, dip a strip of burlap into the plaster and wrap it around the fossil. Repeat until your fossil is covered in plaster strips. It is important to use enough plaster to protect the specimen but not so much that it will be difficult to remove the fossil. Now your "fossil" has a plaster jacket.

5. Set the jacketed fossil on a plastic trash bag to dry. This will take 24 hours.

6. When your jacket is completely dry, you can see what it is like for a paleontologist to open the package. Carefully use a pair of scissors to cut away the jacket. This is exactly what happens when a paleontologist receives a shipment from the field and must remove the jacket to begin studying the fossil.

8

Modern Paleontology

The dawn of the 20th century brought stunning discoveries and new theories to the world of paleontology. Ideas that Mary Anning and William Buckland grappled with were receiving worldwide attention. How old was the Earth? How did climates change over time? Did continents move? What happened to all the dinosaurs? Anning would have been excited to read all the new information science was uncovering.

Dinosaur skulls on display at the British Natural History Museum.
Photo by Darrell Bearce, courtesy of the British Natural History Museum

Marie Curie and Radiometric Dating

Radiometric dating was a discovery that rocked the geological world . . . in a good way. For years paleontologists and geologists argued that the Earth was much older than people imagined. They looked at the evidence of the rock cycle and how long it took for sediment to turn into rock and for fossils to form. They knew it took thousands upon thousands of years, but they had no definitive proof.

In 1902, when Marie Curie detected the phenomenon of radioactivity in uranium, it opened the doors to a new science called *geological radiometric dating*. Radioactive elements are constantly emitting particles of energy called isotopes. This process is called radioactive decay, and it happens at a slow, constant rate. By measuring the amount of decay in an element, scientists can calculate the age of the rock containing that element.

Radiometric dating revolutionized geology and paleontology. In the 1890s some scientists had estimated the world could be nearly 40 million years old. Using radiometric dating, researchers now believe the Earth is over 4 *billion* years old. A planet that was so old would have seen many changes in climate, erosion of hills and mountains, and maybe even shifts in the landmasses of continents.

Marie Curie.
Courtesy of Wikimedia Commons

Alfred Wegener and the Supercontinent Pangea

In 1912, Alfred Wegener proposed a crazy theory that left scientists scratching their heads. Alfred was sure that at one point in time the continents of the Earth had once all been attached together in a huge landmass that he called Pangea. He theorized that the continents were not fixed in place but instead were drifting across the Earth, sometimes even bumping into each other. Wegener said this would explain why he found tropical plant fossils

Popcorn Time Decay

Paleontologists use radiometric dating to establish the age of fossils. The age of rocks can be determined by the amount of time it takes for one radioactive element to decay and turn into another element. The time necessary for half of any given amount of one element to decay and become another element is called the half-life. The original element is called the parent element, and the element that results is called the daughter element.

Scientists often use a form of radiometric dating known as K-Ar geochronology. This involves the element potassium (represented by the chemical symbol K) that is found in volcanic ash. Potassium changes into the element argon (chemical symbol Ar). The half-life of K-Ar is 1.25 billion years. By measuring the ratio of potassium to argon in crystals found in volcanic ash, scientists determine the age of the rocks.

You can experiment with popcorn to help you understand how radioactive decay can be used to measure the passage of time.

MATERIALS

- Permanent markers
- 3 bags of microwavable popcorn
- Microwave
- Stopwatch/timer

1. First, use the marker to label each bag of microwavable popcorn with an amount of time. The bags should be labeled:

   10 seconds

   30 seconds

   50 seconds

2. Put the first bag in the microwave and set the timer for 3 minutes. Get the stopwatch ready and set it for 10 seconds. As the popcorn begins cooking, listen for the kernels to pop. When you hear the first kernel pop, start the stopwatch. When 10 seconds are up, remove the bag of popcorn from the microwave. Set it aside to cool.

3. Repeat the process with each bag of popcorn, increasing the time as listed, 30 seconds and then 50 seconds. The unpopped kernel of corn represents the parent element. Heating the kernel causes the popcorn to "decay," or pop. The resulting popped kernel is the daughter element. As time passes, more of the kernels pop, and more of the parent element turns into the daughter element. In the case of potassium, as time passes, it turns into argon.

4. Now, look at the bags of popcorn. Notice how the number of popped kernels has increased the longer the bag spent in the microwave. The changes in the popcorn mimic what scientists observe in the changes of radioactive elements over different amounts of time.

in the Artic and why tropical dinosaur bones were found in South Africa, India, and Antarctica.

The idea made complete sense to Swiss geologist Émile Argand, who thought the continental collisions were the best explanation for the folded and buckled rock strata he saw in the Swiss Alps. And South African geologist Alexander Du Toit supported the theory because this explained the similarity of the rocks and fossils found in Africa and South America.

But most scholars thought this was ridiculous. Continents didn't move. They stayed in one place.

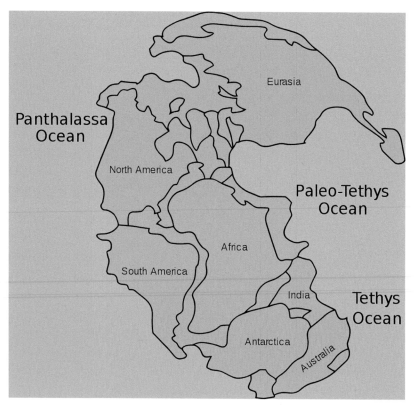

Pangea. *Adrignola, courtesy of the artist, Wikimedia Commons,*
https://commons.wikimedia.org/wiki/File:Pangea_continents_and_oceans.svg

Maybe there were land bridges animals used to get to the other continents, and the bridges fell into the ocean because of earthquakes. One continent? The idea was preposterous! Besides, how long would it take for continents to break apart and drift away from each other? And what caused the movement? Wegener's ideas were ignored.

It wasn't until the 1950s, nearly 20 years after Wegener's death, that scientists started proving his theory was correct. They discovered plate tectonics, the idea that the Earth's surface was made up of constantly moving and sliding plates. Over 200 million years ago, all the continents fit together like a jigsaw puzzle. Today scientists believe that the Earth may have gone through many cycles of one continent breaking into pieces. With a planet that is over 4 billion years old, there's been plenty of time for the continents to drift.

The Alvarez Theory

For decades, scientists, researchers, scholars, and schoolkids have wondered, *What happened to the dinosaurs?* Fossil evidence shows that they ruled the earth for millennia, and then suddenly they were gone. Theories about what happened have ranged from worldwide floods or volcanic eruptions to giant tsunamis or a supernova star explosion. Some scientists believed the dinosaur demise was more gradual and was caused by the increasing dominance of mammals.

Walter Alvarez was a geologist who investigated a strange phenomenon called the K-T boundary. This was a grayish layer of clay found in rock layers all over the world. The layer was unusual because below the clay, the limestone was full of different types of fossils, but above the layer, there were only fossils of one species of a tiny marine animal called foraminifera. It was the same everywhere in the world.

Puzzled at what this could mean, Walter brought samples home to show his father, the famous Nobel-winning scientist Luis Alvarez. Luis was excited. He loved a good science mystery. Luis decided to measure the amount of the radioactive element iridium that was in the K-T layer. This would give an idea of whether the layers were created at the same time or not. The results showed that the K-T was the same age in all areas of the world and that age was 65 million years . . . right about the time the dinosaurs died.

The Alvarezes hypothesized that the K-T layer was the result of a giant asteroid hitting the Earth. The impact sent dust, smoke, and iridium into the atmosphere, blocking the sun and lowering the Earth's temperature. The lack of sunlight and cold temperatures killed the plants that the dinosaurs depended on for food. This collapsed the dinosaur food chain, with plant-eaters dying first, followed by predators and then scavengers. The smaller mammals and birds were the animals that survived, by eating roots and seeds. This meant the end of the dinosaur era and the rise of mammals.

Their hypothesis is still being debated today, but many scientists believe that their theory correlates well with a huge asteroid (or comet) impact site that was discovered in Chicxulub, Mexico. The crater from this impact is 12 miles (20 km)

Walter (right) and Luis Alvarez.
Courtesy of Lawrence Berkeley Laboratory, Wikimedia Commons

deep and spans 93 miles (150 km). It also formed about 65 million years ago.

New Century, More Questions

The 21st century has been good to paleontology. Modern scientific equipment like CT scanners and electron microscopes allow researchers to see inside fossils and learn more about internal

Plate Tectonics

The Earth is made up of many layers. The outermost layer is called the crust. The crust is broken up into very large pieces called tectonic plates, and they fit together like a jigsaw puzzle. These plates float on the mantle layer of the Earth. The mantle can flow like a liquid if it is hot enough and has enough pressure. This liquid mantle allows the plates to move, and sometimes they bump into each other, causing earthquakes and volcanoes and creating mountains.

You can make a model of the Earth's crust and mantle to help you understand how plate tectonics work.

MATERIALS

- Red food coloring
- Canned icing
- Butter knife
- Paper plates
- Box of graham cracker squares
- Water

1. Mix the red food coloring into the can of icing. The icing represents the Earth's mantle.

2. With a butter knife, spread a thick layer of the mantle (icing) on the paper plate.

3. Place two graham crackers on the plate next to each other. The crackers represent the Earth's crust. The line where the crackers meet represents a tectonic plate boundary. There are three types of plate boundaries, and you will demonstrate each one.

4. **Transform Boundary:** this is when two tectonic plates grind against each other, resulting in earthquakes. To demonstrate this, gently push the graham crackers together, then slide them up and down against each other. How does it feel? Do your crackers crumble? This is what happens in areas where plates meet and rub against each other, like on California's San Andreas Fault.

5. **Divergent Boundary:** this occurs when two plates move away from each other. Get a plate of icing and two new crackers. This time press down on the crackers while you pull them apart. Your icing or mantle will erupt up between the two crackers (plates). This represents how two oceanic plates move away from each other. The hot magma from the mantle flows up where the plates separate, forming underwater lava flows that build new seafloor and volcanic islands.

6. **Convergent Boundary:** this happens when two tectonic plates move toward each other. The plates can either *collide*, creating mountains, or one plate can slide under the other at the *subduction* zone, creating volcanoes.

To model a **collision**, you will need a fresh plate of icing and two graham crackers. Dip one edge of each graham cracker in some water. Place them on the icing mantle with the wet sides facing each other. Press the crackers together. The soft crackers will fold up to form "mountains," just as tectonic plates create mountain ranges when they collide.

To model a **subduction zone**, take another plate of icing and two more graham crackers. This time as you slide the crackers together, press one cracker underneath the other. These form a different type of mountain, a volcano, because they allow some of the mantle to flow through. An example is the Cascade Range in the Western United States and Canada.

7. After you've created your plate tectonic models, you can clean up by eating a few mountains and volcanoes.

structures. GPS and satellite imaging give field teams specific information about rock layers and where to plan a dig. Computers, digital cameras, and video allow scientists to record their finds, share information, and consult with colleagues around the world.

All the advancements would have delighted Mary Anning, especially in education. Now universities are open to men and women of all races and socioeconomic backgrounds. Scholarships and grants are available to help students with their financial needs. New equipment and new voices in the field have led to an explosion of research and opportunities.

Jingmai O'Connor.
Courtesy of the subject, Wikimedia Commons

Jingmai O'Connor

Today's paleontologists can choose to work in a variety of specialized areas. Scientist Jingmai O'Connor is a vertebrate paleontologist who works as a curator at the Field Museum in Chicago. O'Connor, who is proud of her Chinese Irish American heritage, did not grow up as a dinosaur fan. What O'Connor enjoyed was tagging along with her geologist mother when she did fieldwork. Collecting rocks and minerals and playing in the lab piqued O'Connor's interest in studying geology.

After graduating with a PhD, O'Connor moved to Beijing and worked at the Institute of Vertebrate Paleontology and Paleoanthropology, studying prehistoric birds and their development. Bird fossils are rare, because their bones are lightweight and delicate, so when they die, their bodies are not usually preserved. So when O'Connor and her team discovered a species of prehistoric bird that had never been seen, the world took notice. Each new fossil helps form a better picture of the ancient life of birds and how they developed. This bird had sharp teeth and clawed fingers on each wing, very different from modern birds. O'Connor named the bird *Qiliania graffini* after Greg Graffin, the lead singer in her favorite punk rock band.

Trowelblazers

The Trowelblazers is an Internet site (https://trowelblazers.com/) that celebrates the achievements of women in the "digging sciences," women who picked up trowels and excavated ichthyosaurs and tyrannosaurs, women who excavated ancient cities, explored Egyptian tombs, dug up fossilized forests, and protected ancient relics in a job that was traditionally considered men's work.

The site was started by four female scientists who noticed that history seemed to leave out the stories and discoveries made by women. Who was going to right this wrong? They were. The creators of Trowelblazers and keepers of women's digging history are:

Brenna Hassett, a bioarcheologist and popular science writer who specializes in ancient teeth. She is the author of two books with more to come.

Tori Herridge, an evolutionary biologist at the Natural History Museum in London and an expert in elephants and mammoths. (She has a special interest in the dwarf variety.) She also presents on podcasts and television.

Suzanne Pilaar Birch, who uses archeology with biogeochemistry to study how humans adapted to climate change in prehistory. She's a professor at the University of Georgia.

Rebecca Wragg Sykes, an archeologist and author who studies human origins and ancient technology. She is an honorary fellow in the School of Archeology, Classics, and Egyptology at the University of Liverpool.

Founded in 2013, the Trowelblazers project is community sourced, meaning the authors not only do their own research but also ask people around the world to supply information about pioneering women archeologists, paleontologists, and geologists. They are particularly interested in collecting stories of underrepresented women with diverse backgrounds who have contributed to the digging sciences.

The Trowelblazers team is dedicated to excavating the hidden workers and citizen scientists like Yusura, a Palestinian village woman who in 1932 was assisting archeologist Dorothy Garrod with a dig on Mount Carmel and discovered the skull of a female Neanderthal known as Tabun 1. Yusura supervised the dig site for six years, acting as the forewoman, but her story along with her last name has been lost to history. The Trowelblazers dug through archives and field notes to uncover her story and give her proper credit for the discovery of Tabun 1, one of the most important human fossils ever found.

The story of Gussie White and the excavation of the Irene Mound in Savannah, Georgia, was publicized by the Trowelblazers. Between the years 1937 and 1940, 32 white women and over 80 African American women were employed by the US government to excavate a Native American settlement. The jobs were part of a recovery program designed to provide work for women whose husbands were unemployed during the Great Depression. The women were responsible for everything from digging trenches and surveying to analyzing human remains. The stories of the white women

Citizen Science

You don't have to have a college degree to do science. Mary Anning taught herself about anatomy and made significant contributions to the young science of paleontology. Today scientists work with kids and adults around the world to gain information and conduct experiments. The people helping researchers are called citizen scientists, *and they assist in making discoveries every year.*

You can become involved as a citizen scientist. There is a database where scientists list the projects that they need help with. You can participate in projects to help astronauts develop a machine learning model to identify uncategorized geographic features, or you can help park rangers track invading plant and animal species. There are hundreds of projects that need help from citizen scientists just like you!

It's easy to become a citizen scientist. All you will need to get started is your legal guardian's permission and a computer. The Citizen Science clearinghouse lists hundreds of projects. Go to https://www.citizenscience.gov/catalog/# to begin your career as a citizen scientist.

Examples of science projects include:

- Tracking seasonal changes in flora and fauna on the Appalachian Trail
- Participating in the annual Christmas bird count
- Understanding the climate changes in the Arctic
- Researching kelp forests
- Learning archeology and excavation techniques
- Monitoring the American pika population
- Assessing coastal change due to storms and weather

who participated are well documented, but very little is known about the African American women.

Gussie White was one of the few Black workers whose story is remembered. She was trained as an educator before the Great Depression and took the job when her husband was disabled. Her work uncovered important cultural artifacts and led to new information about the life of Native Americans. Like Mary Anning, Gussie White's work would be forgotten if it were not for the conscientious work of people like the Trowelblazers to preserve their history.

Paleoecology

Mary Anning and William Buckland were the first people who studied prehistoric coprolites. They understood that the way to learn about an animal was to investigate its poop. Karen Chin agrees.

As a paleoecologist she studies the interactions between extinct organisms and the environments where they lived. Chin has learned a great deal about dinosaurs from the study of their feces, including the fact that dinosaurs had worms living in their intestines. She also knows that tyrannosaurs were not delicate eaters. They chomped down their food quickly and often ingested pieces of bone, which she has found in coprolites. She has also seen pieces of fossilized muscle tissue preserved inside a tyrannosaur coprolite. Fossilized poop helps explain how prehistoric animals lived and what they ate and hunted.

Chin spent many summers working as an interpretive ranger in national parks. Leading nature walks taught her the value of animal scat and the information it contained. Today Chin holds a PhD from the University of California, Santa Barbara and is a professor and curator of paleontology at the University of Colorado Boulder, where she continues to study coprolites to better understand ancient ecosystems.

Paleobiology

Paleobiologists like Lauren Sallan study more than the fossilized remains of animals; their research may include any biological system. They examine ancient plant fossils, fossilized bacteria, and single-cell animals to better understand the molecular evolution and history of life. They can even analyze DNA and RNA samples when they are available.

With a PhD from the University of Chicago, Sallan has done studies into how species survive mass extinctions. Her research has shown that smaller animals tend to survive catastrophic events better than animals with large bodies. Smaller bodies require fewer nutrients to maintain life and can reproduce quickly.

This evidence helps ecologists today, because overfishing is making the environment unstable. Scientists need to know how or if the ecosystem

(left) **Karen Chin.**
Courtesy of the National Park Service, Wikimedia Commons

(right) **Lauren Sallan.**
Courtesy of the subject, Wikimedia Commons, https://commons.wikimedia .org/wiki/File:SallanCommencement _(cropped).jpg

can recover and what humans can do to help. Researching mass extinction in the past gives clues on how to deal with today's problems.

Paleontology's Importance

During Mary Anning's lifetime, scientists were discovering animals that lived long before humans came into existence. Scholars were confronted with the idea of animal extinction for the very first time.

Now science believes there have been at least five mass extinction events in history. We are now experiencing conditions on Earth that could lead to another one. This time the threat is not a volcanic explosion or a huge asteroid; instead, it is the human impact on the environment. In what's known as a *biodiversity crisis*, nearly a million species are threatened due to deforestation, invasive species, disease, pollution, overfishing, and hunting.

The knowledge that paleontologists gain from studying the past can give scientists ideas on how to lessen the problems of today. The study of extinct and fossilized life-forms may very well help preserve modern animal species. Paleontologists' studies of the past can directly impact the future of the Earth.

How to Become a Paleontologist

Do you long to dig for dinosaur bones? Can you imagine traveling around the world climbing mountains and scouring deserts searching for the skeleton of an animal no human has seen before? It's like being a treasure hunter, but instead of a chest of gold, your treasure is teeth, claws, skulls, and other bones. This is the life of a paleontologist—full of excitement, discovery, and hard work.

Like Mary Anning, modern paleontologists do fieldwork, searching for and excavating fossilized plants and animals. But fieldwork is only part of the job. They also spend time in laboratories examining their finds under powerful microscopes, conducting chemical and biological tests, writing reports, and communicating with other scientists. It's a career full of variety and adventure, but it takes planning to make the dream a reality.

The first requirement for becoming a paleontologist is to be curious about the world around you. Ask questions about how nature works. How are animals similar and different? Why do some plants thrive while others die? How do humans impact the environment?

Then work to learn the answers. Visit museums, national parks, and science centers. Take biology, ecology, chemistry, physics, and advanced math classes in high school. This will prepare you for your university program. To gain practical experience with fossils, you can join a geology club or volunteer at a local museum.

If you want to become a paleontologist, you will need an advanced college degree. After graduating from high school, you'll need to pursue a bachelor of science degree with a concentration in both biology and geology. You will also need

Make Fake Amber Resin Fossils

Resin—sometimes called sap—is a fluid produced by trees to help the tree heal when it is cut or injured. The resin is thick and sticky. It attracts insects and small animals that can get stuck in the resin and die.

Amber is a prehistoric tree resin that has hardened into a rock. It can be many colors, including red, yellow, and green. Any animal that is trapped in the resin is perfectly preserved, so amber is highly prized by fossil hunters and paleontologists.

You can experiment to learn how amber is made.

MATERIALS

* Modeling clay
* Yellow and red food coloring
* Clear resin (available at hardware stores)
* Stirring stick
* Dead insect—you can find them in light fixtures or windowsills, or use plastic insects
* Journal

1. Make a ball of modeling clay the size of a baseball. Then press down into the clay ball with your thumb, creating a hole that goes about halfway through the ball.

2. Push the ball down into your work surface so that it has a flat base and can stand up on its own.

3. Mix several drops of red or yellow food coloring into your clear resin with a stirring stick, to mimic the color of amber.

4. Fill half of the hole in your clay ball with resin. Then place your dead or plastic insect into the resin. Fill the hole the rest of the way with the resin. Let it dry for at least 24 hours.

5. When the resin is dry, peel away the clay and you will have an amber fossil.

6. You can examine your fossil under the microscope just like a paleontologist. Record your observations in your journal.

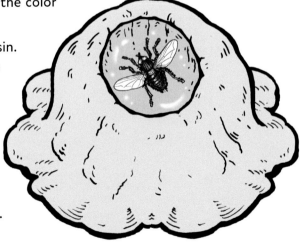

to take courses in writing, history, math, and languages. During the summers you should find internships for fieldwork experiences. Many museums, universities, and national parks have field programs where students learn how to excavate prehistoric plants and animals.

Most jobs in paleontology require an advanced degree. This means you will need to earn a doctorate (PhD). During your graduate studies you will work with a professor to learn more about lab work and decide on one of the following specialty areas:

Vertebrate paleontology: the study of fossils of animals with backbones.

Invertebrate paleontology: the study of fossils of animals without backbones.

Micropaleontology: the study of very small fossils that require the use of microscopes.

Paleobotany: the study of plant fossils.

Taphonomy: the study of how fossils form and are preserved.

Biostratigraphy: the study of the vertical distribution of fossils in rocks.

Paleoecology: the study of ancient ecosystems and how they developed.

Conservation paleobiology: the study of geological records that provides a long-term perspective on modern conservation and restoration issues.

Once you have obtained your PhD, you will be ready to go to work as a museum curator, college professor, research scientist, science writer, or geological mapper.

Who knows, you may discover a new species of dinosaur and get to be the person who names it.

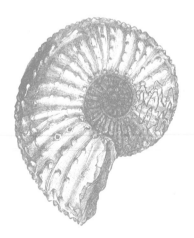

Glossary

anatomist A specialist in the study of animal bodies.

articulating Putting together the bones of a skeleton in a way that shows the natural connections between the bones and how they work in the body.

carnivore A creature that feeds on other animals.

cave A natural underground chamber typically located on a cliff or hillside that is large enough for a human to enter.

cephalopod Any mollusk belonging to the class Cephalopoda, which have tentacles attached to their head. They include cuttlefish, squid, and octopuses.

coprolites The fossilized waste matter of animals. Also known as *bezoar stones*.

dinosaur Any of the ancient reptiles of the Mesozoic Era that belong to the Dinosauria group.

Earth's crust The outer layer of the Earth that is made up of rocks and minerals.

fossil Any indication of ancient life. Most fossils are from the hard parts of life-forms, such as teeth, bones, or shells in animals or wood in plants. Preserved trackways, burrows, and footprints are also considered fossils.

fossilization The process by which the remains of ancient living things are turned into rock.

glacier A massive sheet of ice that slowly creeps over the land, scraping it bare. As the ice sheet retreats (melts), the glacier will leave behind deposits of sand and gravel.

igneous rock Rock that is formed through the cooling and solidification of magma or lava.

invertebrates A group of animals that lack backbones.

Mesozoic Era The Age of Reptiles (Dinosaurs)—the second era since complex life appeared on earth—from 225 to 65 million years ago.

metamorphic rock Rocks that are formed when other rocks are changed due to heat or pressure.

mold The impression a shell or other organic object leaves in the sediment. If the mold preserves the outer structure of the object, then it is an *external mold*. If the mold preserves the internal structure of the object, then it is an *internal mold*.

mosasaurs Group of marine reptiles.

paleontologist One who studies fossils.

petrified Having turned to stone or a stony substance.

plate tectonics The theory that the surface of the Earth is made up of constantly moving and sliding plates, whose motion causes earthquakes and volcanoes and, over millions of years, creates mountains and reshapes the continents.

pterosaur Any of the flying reptiles of the Mesozoic Era.

roadcut A deep slice in the ground created by blasting through a hill or mountain. The process is used to create level streets or to expose layers of rock so they can be studied by scientists.

sedimentary rock Rock made of layers of tightly packed sand and clay.

species A group of very closely related life-forms.

strata map A geological map that shows the different layers of rock formation in an area.

topography The physical appearance of the natural features of an area, especially the shape of its surface.

trace fossil A fossilized sign that a plant or animal once lived in an area (e.g., footprints, coprolite).

vertebra One of the series of bones that make up the spine. Plural: *vertebrae.*

vertebrates A group of animals that possess backbones.

Resources

———

Learn more about Mary Anning and paleontology by exploring these resources.

Places to Visit

American Museum of Natural History
200 Central Park West
New York, NY 10024-5102
212-769-5100
www.amnh.org
The American Museum of Natural History is home to over 600 fossil specimens, and 100 of those are dinosaurs.

Arizona Museum of Natural History
53 N. MacDonald
Mesa, AZ 85201
408-644-2230
www.arizonamuseumofnaturalhistory.org
The Dinosaur Mountain exhibit allows visitors to experience a realistic Mesozoic Era with animatronic dinosaurs and a live-action waterfall and flood.

Children's Museum of Indianapolis
3000 N. Meridian St.
Indianapolis, IN 46208-4716
317-334-4000
www.childrensmuseum.org
The world's largest children's museum with over 1 million visitors yearly. Visitors can visit a dinosaur habitat from the Cretaceous Period and learn about the science of paleontology.

Dickinson Museum Center
188 Museum Dr. East
Dickinson, ND 58601
701-456-6225
http://dickinsonmuseumcenter.com/badlands_exhibits/
The Dickinson Museum Center houses an impressive collection of fossils and minerals, including the skeletons of *Stegosaurus*, *Allosaurus*, and *Triceratops*.

Field Museum of Natural History

1400 S. Lake Shore Dr.

Chicago, IL 60605

312-922-9410

www.fieldmuseum.org

Known for being the home of the famous *T. rex* Sue, the most complete and largest *T. rex* skeleton ever discovered.

Houston Museum of Natural Science

5555 Hermann Park Dr.

Houston, TX 77030

713-639-4629

www.hmns.org

Step into a world where dinosaurs roam the earth. A unique 30-minute holographic movie allows viewers to feel as if they are sharing the same space with prehistoric giants. This educational journey helps the audience gain a deeper understanding of dinosaurs' adaptations and habitats.

Museum of the Rockies

600 W. Kagy Blvd.

Bozeman, MT 59717

404-994-2251

https://museumoftherockies.org/

Visit the Siebel Dinosaur Complex and explore exhibits like Dinosaurs Under the Big Sky and Landforms/Lifeforms. You'll meet an impressive *T. rex* sculpture named Big Mike and an *Allosaurus* skeleton named Big Al.

Smithsonian National Museum of Natural History

10th St. & Constitution Ave. NW

Washington, DC 20560

202-633-1000

https://naturalhistory.si.edu/

Exhibits of rare fossils, minerals, gemstones, and 46 complete specimens of dinosaurs are all available to visitors free of charge.

Websites to Explore

British Natural History Museum

https://www.nhm.ac.uk/discover.html

This site is run by the museum and has scientific news including new paleontological discoveries from around the world. You can view some of the fossils Mary Anning excavated.

Digital Atlas of Ancient Life

https://www.digitalatlasofancientlife.org/vc/

Full of fossil pictures, field guides, and a 3-D view of a *T. rex* skull, this is a great place to learn how to identify fossils. The site was created and is maintained by the Paleontological Research Institution.

DinoBuzz

https://ucmp.berkeley.edu/diapsids/dinobuzz.html

University of California, Berkeley website teaching kids about the science behind dinosaurs.

Dinosaur Database

https://dinosaurpictures.org/

This website has an extensive list of dinosaur names, pictures, and facts from all over the world. The database was created by a collective of paleontologists and includes high-quality, realistic illustrations of prehistoric animals.

Fossils and Paleontology

https://www.nps.gov/subjects/fossils/dinosaurs.htm

Detailed information about the history of paleontology with information about the latest discoveries. Written and maintained by the National Park Service.

Fossils for Kids

http://fossilsforkids.com/

An interactive website dedicated to providing fossil education to kids of all ages. There is information on fossil collecting sites in the US.

Fossils of the Jurassic Coast

https://jurassiccoast.org/what-is-the-jurassic-coast/all-about-fossils/fossils-of-the-jurassic-coast/

Discover the coast where Mary Anning and her contemporaries made their discoveries. The Jurassic Coast Trust provides a website full of news, photos, and information for anyone who loves fossils.

Grand Canyon—National Park Service

https://www.nps.gov/grca/learn/nature/fossils.htm

Learn about the ancient animals that lived in the Grand Canyon. Watch videos and examine 3D images.

La Brea Tar Pits

https://tarpits.org/experience-tar-pits/excavations

Watch a video about fossil excavations and learn how scientists at California's La Brea Tar Pits have recovered over 3.5 million fossils.

Lyme Regis Museum

https://www.lymeregismuseum.co.uk/

Learn about the town where Mary Anning lived and worked. See samples of the types of fossil she collected and try some of the arts and crafts activities.

Museum of the Earth

https://www.museumoftheearth.org/daring-to-dig

Learn about the history of women in paleontology and meet scientists like Devapriya Chattopadhyay, who works in India, and Camila Martínez Aguillón, from Colombia.

National Geographic Kids

https://kids.nationalgeographic.com/animals/prehistoric/

Website designed by the folks at National Geographic. Full of fascinating facts and the latest science news.

Ology Home

https://www.amnh.org/explore/ology/paleontology

A paleontology site for kids run by the American Museum of Natural History.

Paleontological Research Institution

www.priweb.org

The Paleontological Research Institution has teamed up with the Museum of the Earth, the Cayuga Nature Center, and Earth@Home to present a website that has educational videos, reading material, and current research.

ThoughtCo

https://www.thoughtco.com/what-are-fossils-1440576

A reference site with expert-created education content. You can learn about the science of fossils and the latest discoveries and technology.

Books to Read

Dinosaur Lady: The Daring Discoveries of Mary Anning, the First Paleontologist, by Linda Skeers (Sourcebooks, 2020).

Finding Wonders: Three Girls Who Changed Science, by Jeannine Atkins (Atheneum Books for Young Readers, 2017).

Fossil Hunter: How Mary Anning Changed the Science of Prehistoric Life, by Cheryl Blackford (Clarion Books, 2022).

Fossils for Kids: An Introduction to Paleontology, by Dan R. Lynch (Adventure Publications, 2020).

Notes

2. DISCOVERY OF DINOSAURS

"quite upset" her: Mary Anning, letter to Charlotte Murchison, October 11, 1833, Geological Society Archives, LDGSL/838/A/7/3, Natural History Museum Library, London.

3. PROFESSIONAL FOSSILIST

"The fact is that I am": J. A. Cooper, ed., *The Unpublished Journal of Gideon Mantell 1819–1852* (Brighton and Hove, UK: The Royal Pavilion & Museums, 2010), 28–34; Tom Sharpe, *The Fossil Woman: A Life of Mary Anning* (Stanbridge, UK: Dovecote), 141.

"Productive as the coast of Dorsetshire": "Varieties, Literary and Philisophical," *The Monthly Magazine or British Register (of Politics, Literature, and the Belles Lettres)*, vol. 51 (London: Sir Richard Phillips, 1821), 553.

"To the head of a Lizard": William Buckland, *Geology and Mineralogy Considered with Reference to Natural Theology* (London: William Pickering, 1836), 168.

4. A LASTING LEGACY

"We fell in with a shop" and *"I was anxious"*: Carl Gustav Carus, *The King of Saxony's Journey Through England and Scotland in the Year 1844* (London: Chapman and Hall, 1846), 197.

"hardly distinguish the difference": Mary Anning's letters to Charlotte Murchison are housed in the Geological Society Archives, LDGSL/838/A/7/1-3.

"the most beautiful fossil": Mary Anning to William Buckland, December 21, 1830, quoted in W. D. Lang, "Mary Anning and the Pioneer Geologists of Lyme," *Proceedings of the Dorset Natural History and Archaeological Society* 60 (1939): 142–146.

"Oct 5, at Lyme Regis": *Taunton Courier and Western Advertiser*, October 19, 1842, 7.

"There are those among us": Henry de la Beche, "Anniversary Address of the President" in *Quarterly Journal of the Geological Society of London*, vol. 4 (London: Longman, Brown, Green, and Longmans, 1848), xxv.

"This window is sacred": Sharpe, *The Fossil Woman*, 146.

"I propose to call it": Robert Broom, "On a New Type of Mammal-Like Reptile from the South African Karroo Beds (Anningia megalops)," *Proceedings of the Zoological Society of London* 97 (1927): 227–232.

5. WILLIAM AND MARY BUCKLAND

"It must already appear": William Buckland, *Reliquiæ Diluvianæ* (London: John Murray, 1823), 19–20, accessed December 12, 2022, Wellcome Collection, https://wellcomecollection.org/works/k7twatkd.

"Dr. Buckland was once": Caroline Fox, "October 8, 1938," *Memories of Old Friends: Being Extracts from the Journals and Letters of Caroline Fox of Penjerrick, Cornwall, from 1835 to 1871*, ed. Horace N. Pym (London: Smith, Elder, 1882), 44.

Author reading Mary Anning's letters in the archives of the British Natural History Museum. *Photo by Darrell Bearce, courtesy of the photographer*

Index

Page numbers in **bold** *refer to images*

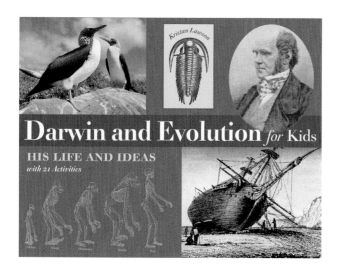

ISBN 978-1-55652-502-5

$19.99 (CAN $25.99)

Darwin and Evolution for Kids
His Life and Ideas with 21 Activities

KRISTAN LAWSON

An NSTA-CBC Outstanding Science Trade Books for Students K–12 Selection

When Charles Darwin left England in 1831 aboard the HMS *Beagle*, he never expected his voyage would change the way humans viewed the world—the 22-year-old was looking for adventure! As the ship's naturalist, he was hired on to collect specimens of animals, plants, and fossils from faraway lands and ship them back to England for study, and to write about what he observed. The two-year voyage turned into five, and by the time he returned home, he was a national celebrity. *Darwin and Evolution for Kids* traces the transformation of a privileged and somewhat scatterbrained youth into the great thinker who proposed the revolutionary theory he called the Transmutation of Species Through Natural Selection, what most people now call the Theory of Evolution. By encouraging readers to define the differences between theories and beliefs, facts and opinions, *Darwin and Evolution for Kids* does not shy away from a concept that continues to spark heated public debate more than a century after it was first proposed.

Darwin's voyage and ideas are explored through engaging and fun activities where children can:

- Make their own **fossils** using clay, seashells, and plaster
- Keep **field notes** as backyard naturalists
- Investigate whether **acquired traits** are passed along to future generations
- Explore the various **adaptive strategies** plants have developed to distribute seeds
- Observe how **carnivorous plants** trap and devour their prey
- Go on a **botanical treasure hunt**